# Teen Pregnancy

Look for these and other books in the Lucent
Overview Series:

Teen Alcoholism
Teen Depression
Teen Dropouts
Teen Drug Abuse
Teen Eating Disorders
Teen Parenting
Teen Prostitution
Teens and Divorce
Teens and Drunk Driving
Teen Sexuality
Teen Smoking
Teen Suicide
Teen Violence

# Teen Pregnancy

by Patrice Cassedy

TEEN ISSUES

LUCENT Overview Series

**Library of Congress Cataloging-in-Publication Data**

Cassedy, Patrice, 1953–
    Teen pregnancy / by Patrice Cassedy.
        p.   cm. — (Teen issues)
    Includes bibliographical references and index.
    Summary: Discusses the social causes of teen pregnancy, problems
faced by pregnant teens and the alternatives available to them, the impact
of parenthood on teens of both sexes, and approaches to the problem.
    ISBN 1-56006-515-X (acid-free)
    1. Teenage pregnancy—Juvenile literature.  2. Teenage mothers—
Juvenile literature.  [1. Pregnancy.  2. Teenage mothers.  3. Adoption.
4. Abortion.]  I. Title.  II. Series.
HQ759.4 .C37  2002
306.7'0835—dc21
                                           2001001692

# Contents

# Introduction

A 1998 ARTICLE in the *New York Times* bore the headline: "Fewer Teen-Age Mothers? Maybe. In Los Angeles, They're Skeptical." The article was written in response to a report from statisticians: In 1998 teen birth rates in the United States were down about 18 percent from the 1991 rate. The journalist, Don Terry, took the news to the streets of Los Angeles to see what teenagers thought.

Some were doubtful that any improvement in the rate of teen pregnancy had been made. "More of my friends have been getting pregnant than not," one nineteen-year-old girl told Terry, adding, "It's just me and two of my friends who aren't pregnant and who don't have any kids."[1] But teens who accepted the validity of Terry's information used their experiences and observations to suggest what might have taken place to make the change. Most believed it was due to an increased use of condoms (based more on a fear of AIDS than to prevent pregnancy). Some teens pointed to more abortions as a cause, while others expressed their own determination to avoid sex because they planned to enjoy childhood as children, not parents, or had ambitions to attend college.

## Good news . . . and bad

While teens, commentators, politicians, parents, and educators have various theories on why the birth rate among teens is down, the trend is welcome. Hand in hand with the decline in teen birth rates is a decline in teen pregnancy. Between 1991 and 1996, 15 percent fewer pregnancies occurred among young women fifteen to nineteen years old. Nevertheless, even after this change, the United States Centers for Disease Control and Prevention reports that about one million teenagers become pregnant each year.

## Hard choices

A girl who suspects she is pregnant will almost certainly experience worry and fear. The emotions surrounding this worry are portrayed in the true diary *It Happened to Nancy*. In this excerpt, the pseudonymous teenage author reacts to her friend's fears about the significance of a late menstrual period:

> Dorie still hasn't had her period. That's scary. She's used those little packages that come out pink if you are . . . and it's pink or vice versa. We were all so upset about her . . . I'm really glad I'm not her! I don't know what I'd do either. She says she decides one thing one day and then changes her mind the next. . . . It's a horrible decision either way, and she's only got weeks to decide if she's going to have an abortion. That would be soooo hard . . . I would never, never, never give [my baby] up. . . . But what would I do? I'm just fifteen years old. Who would tend the baby? Would I have to live with my mother forever? Would I have to quit school?[2]

If a suspected pregnancy is confirmed, the girl faces difficult decisions, often without the support of those she would ordinarily turn to for advice. In whom does she confide? How does she balance her needs and fears against her beliefs about abortion versus adoption versus teen parenting? What should the role of the father be? Is marriage a realistic option? What about single motherhood? If she chooses abortion, who will pay for it? How will she feel afterward? And, since more than half the states require parental involvement when a minor seeks an abortion, how will she tell her parents?

Although numbers alone do not tell the very personal stories of individual teens, they do give insight into the American teen response to pregnancy. In the United States, more than half of pregnant teens decide to have their babies, and about one-third opt for abortions. (Another 14 percent lose their babies through miscarriages.) Among

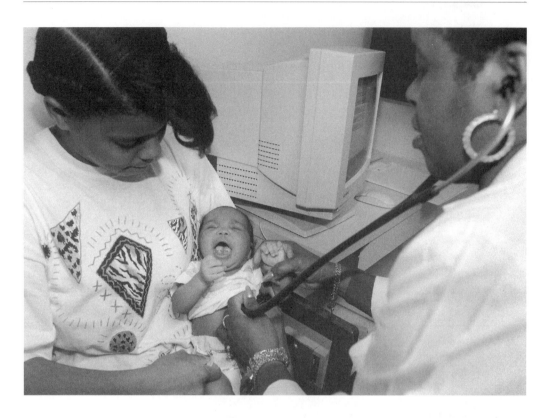

*Many teens who become pregnant decide to keep their babies.*

teenage girls who give birth, nearly 80 percent are unmarried. A small minority of all girls who give birth—less than 1 percent according to 1995 estimates published by the National Adoption Information Clearinghouse—place their babies through adoption, while the others raise children with varying degrees of support from the father and family. Since so much is at state, these choices inevitably lead to worry and stress for the pregnant teen.

## "Mom, I'm pregnant"

Reporter Cynthia Hanson documented the choices of three pregnant teens in an article for *Ladies' Home Journal.* Taking the perspective of the girls' mothers, she began her article by stating the obvious: "When your daughter is a teenager and unmarried . . . [Mom, I'm pregnant] are the three words you pray you'll never hear."[3] She went on to detail how each pregnant teen, with her mother's involvement, selected a course of action and carried it through.

Eighteen-year-old Nicole chose to keep her baby, and with the support of her mother, Sharon, she and her boyfriend continued their educations and eventually married. With a five-year-old granddaughter to admire, Sharon expressed her gratitude that Nicole chose to keep her baby. Nevertheless, Sharon was not without regrets: "Nicole and Michael are great parents, and they've got their priorities straight. But it still makes me sad that they didn't get to be kids."[4]

*Although some teens find parenting a positive experience, they miss out on many typical teen activities.*

Another pregnant teen, fifteen-year-old Krystle, decided on open adoption, where she would be permitted to keep in touch with, and visit, the child. Hanson reported that Krystle and her mother, Jan, found it difficult to stick with the decision once ten-pound-eight-ounce Abigail Rose was born. They were highly emotional when finally faced with the reality of their choice. But, believing that Abigail's life would be better with her adoptive parents, they went forward. As Jan reflected later, "Krystle misses seeing Abby grow up each day. But we're thrilled that Abby is happy, and we're glad to be a part of her extended family. I know we did the right thing."[5]

Helen (whose name was changed for the article), a student at an all-girl high school, decided to undergo a medical abortion, a procedure that can only be used in the earliest stages of pregnancy. Helen reported feeling terrible about the circumstances of becoming pregnant before marriage, but did not have second thoughts about the procedure. After high school she completed four years of college and went on to pursue a master's degree. When Hanson asked Helen's mother to reflect on the decision, she replied, "If Helen had had the baby, she would be leading a different life now. It wouldn't have been the path that I would have chosen—and not the one she had in her dreams. For her, abortion was the only solution."[6]

## A hot topic

While a focus on the stories of Nicole, Krystle, and Helen casts the issue in terms of individual decisions, teen pregnancy is anything but a purely personal topic. In fact, teen pregnancy is a "hot" topic in America, not only because of the impact on babies born to (or those fetuses aborted by) teens, but also because society as a whole bears the weight of the problem. Many solutions have been proposed and implemented and, judging from current trends, some are working. But the debate over teen pregnancy—a reality of human life that comes with high personal and societal costs—will long continue in political, religious, educational, legal, and personal settings.

# 1

# The Problem with Teen Pregnancy

WHEN AMERICANS SPEAK about "teen pregnancy" they are invariably referring to the *problem* of teen pregnancy. The concern over teen pregnancy is so great in this country that the federal government allotted $50 million each year from 1998 to 2002 to fund programs to teach abstinence. Indeed, in 1998 and 1999 the federal government and some of the states cofunded 698 new programs.

In addition to these programs, government policymakers, private foundations, school administrators, doctors, religious leaders, teachers, and parents intensely debate the causes of teen pregnancy and discuss ways to reduce it.

## Personal responsibility

Of course, teens themselves are not excluded as subjects of this debate. The National Campaign to Prevent Teen Pregnancy (a nonprofit, nonpartisan organization that works to reduce teen pregnancy rates) reports that 95 percent of American adults and 85 percent of teenagers believe that society should encourage teens to stay abstinent (not have intercourse) at least through high school. The campaign also reports that nearly 60 percent of adults also support making birth control available to teens who decide against abstinence and become sexually active. Almost universally there is a sense that teens must take responsibility for developing mature ways of handling their sexuality: either by abstaining or by taking appropriate birth

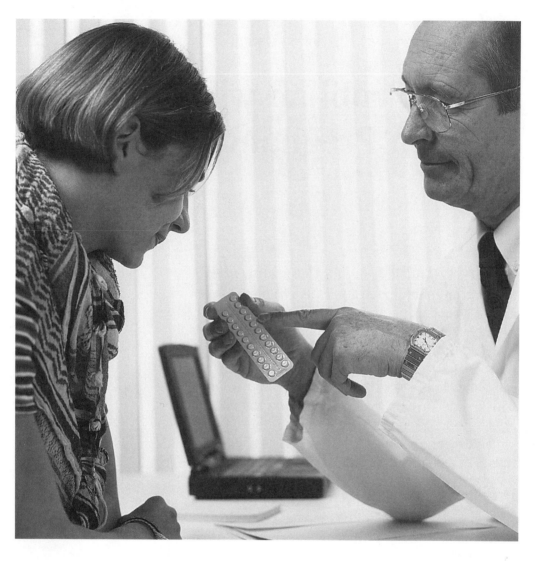

*A doctor discusses contraception with a teen. Many Americans feel that teens must take responsibility for their sexuality, either through abstinence or by using birth control.*

control measures. Even beyond this challenge of preventing unwanted pregnancies, there exists the problem of a small but significant population of teenagers who, for a number of complicated reasons, set out to become parents.

Although sexual activity leading to pregnancy and birth is vital to human existence, it is clear that American society as a whole is strongly opposed to *teen* pregnancy. This societal attitude results on the one hand from moral and religious disapproval of sexual activity among unmarried teens. On the other hand, true-life examples and statistical data show that pregnancies in the teen population exact heavy societal, economic, personal, and health tolls.

## Health risks to teens

Whether or not a girl becomes pregnant, sexual activity can create health problems for females and males alike. Every year, one in four sexually experienced teens, a percentage that translates into three million young people, catches a sexually transmitted disease (STD). STDs are passed from one person to another through intimate sexual contact. Some of these diseases can be spread through unprotected vaginal, anal, or oral sex. Other STDs can be spread through sexual contact that includes kissing or skin-to-skin contact. There are more than thirty types of STDs. The most common STDs include genital herpes (fluid-filled blisters); human papillomavirus (genital warts); other serious infections such as gonorrhea, chlamydia, syphilis, and trichomoniasis; and hepatitis B, which can damage the liver. The human immune deficiency virus (HIV), which can lead to AIDS, can also be passed on to a partner through sexual activity.

The United States Centers for Disease Control and Prevention and other health organizations stress that if people use latex condoms or vaginal pouches every time they have oral, anal, or vaginal intercourse, they significantly reduce their risk of catching STDs. However, even these methods are not completely safe. Condoms can break or leak. In addition, condoms and vaginal pouches do not always isolate the germs that cause certain STDs, including hepatitis B, herpes, and human papillomavirus.

The Planned Parenthood Federation of America (which provides information and services related to sexuality and family planning, and lobbies to support the freedom to use birth control and choose abortion) explains the seriousness of these diseases as follows: "While a few [STD] infections are only unpleasant, many have dangerous consequences and require professional medical treatment. Some can cause sterility. Others can affect a developing fetus or newborn and may cause birth defects. Some increase the risk of getting certain cancers. And others, such as hepatitis B, syphilis, and HIV (human immunodeficiency virus) that can cause AIDS, can kill you."[7]

## AIDS

HIV is the most feared of all STDs—with good reason. As the United States Centers for Disease Control and Prevention (CDC) reports, "[s]ince 1992, scientists have estimated that about half the people with HIV develop AIDS [acquired immune deficiency syndrome] within 10 years after becoming infected. This time varies greatly from person to person and can depend on many factors, including a person's health status and their health-related behaviors."[8]

*Education about AIDS is critical, since HIV, which can lead to AIDS, is highly infectious and can be transmitted during unprotected sex.*

Editor Beatrice Sparks summarized the destructive power of AIDS in the epilogue in *It Happened to Nancy*, the pseudonymous diary of a fourteen-year-old girl who died from an HIV infection resulting from a date rape:

Today, as far as professionals know, AIDS is always fatal. Most people with it die within two years of their HIV having advanced to AIDS diagnosis; however, infected people react differently. Some test positive for HIV but go on for years without symptoms. Some people who are infected get very sick right away and die within a short time. Others drift back and forth between health and sickness.[9]

According to the CDC, HIV and AIDS are the sixth leading cause of death among fifteen to twenty-four-year-olds. In 1998 nearly thirty-five hundred teens (age thirteen to nineteen) were diagnosed with AIDS.

Teens have responded to their fear of AIDS by using condoms more often than ever before. Studies show that since 1991, condom use among sexually active teens has increased from 46 to 57 percent. Health experts welcome this trend because using a condom is the best way for sexual partners to avoid transmission of AIDS. Even so, condoms can fail. As Sparks explains, "[Because it may leak or break, even] a latex condom with a spermicide is not 100 percent safe 100 percent of the time."[10]

## Testing is important

HIV is highly infectious. Once HIV is acquired, the newly infected person is immediately a risk to others. Sparks writes in capital letters to emphasize this point: ". . . IF ONE HAS SEXUAL CONTACT WITH AN HIV-INFECTED PERSON ON FRIDAY NIGHT, AND BECOMES INFECTED, HE OR SHE CAN PASS THAT INFECTION ON TO SOMEONE ELSE ON SATURDAY—OR EVEN LATER THAT SAME DAY."[11]

Medical experts agree that a person of any age who suspects that they have been infected with HIV, or with any STD, should immediately stop all sexual contact and seek testing and, if necessary, treatment. While most STDs give off warning signs—painful urination or unusual discharge, soreness, itching, growths, rashes, or blisters in the area of the penis or vagina—HIV is hard to detect until it reaches an advanced stage years after the original infection. Planned Parenthood's "teenwire" website explains to teens why HIV testing is therefore important:

16

> There are a lot of reasons that people get tested for HIV.
> Maybe you're sexually active, and have engaged in risky be-
> havior. Maybe you're in a new relationship and have decided
> to be tested together. The reasons vary from person to person.
>
> In the end, though, it's an important way to take responsibility
> for your life. Finding out that you're negative can be a huge re-
> lief. And if you're positive . . . well . . . the earlier you know,
> the better treatment works and the healthier you can stay.
>
> The guidelines are pretty simple: if you've had unprotected
> sex or have engaged in high-risk behaviors with anyone
> whose sexual history you don't know for sure, or if you or
> any sex partner is an I.V. drug user, you should strongly con-
> sider getting tested.[12]

Testing for STDs and HIV is conducted at community health departments, family planning clinics, hospitals, and doctors' offices. In general, because lawmakers worry that teens will not seek testing unless they can do so confidentially, parental consent is not required. However, some states allow physicians to decide if parents should be notified, and at least one state requires that parents be notified if their child has a positive HIV test.

## Risks of pregnancy

Pregnancy itself creates health risks that can be serious for teenage girls. According to the National Campaign to Prevent Teen Pregnancy, young adolescents (especially those under age fifteen) are two and a half times more likely to die giving birth compared to mothers in their early twenties. Teen mothers also have a greater chance of encountering potentially serious medical problems for the mother and child, including poor weight gain, pregnancy-induced hypertension (high blood pressure), and anemia.

Commentators debate the reasons teenage girls are more likely to experience health problems in pregnancy, and some believe that better health care for teens could close the gap. Author and sociologist Kristin Luker asserts that being a young mother (fifteen and older), in itself does not create maternal or neonatal (newborn) health problems. Rather, statistics "indicate that a very large proportion of the health risks associated with early childbearing are the product of a fragmented and inadequate medical-care system and not of [physical] immaturity."[13]

Providing affordable medical care for all citizens is an urgent issue for politicians and health care experts. Health care is expensive, and unless they have some sort of health insurance or government subsidy to pay for their medical care, many people cannot afford even basic health services. This problem has a significant effect on pregnant teens and their children because they are even more likely to be uninsured than the rest of the population. For example, while 15.5 percent of the U.S. population has no insurance to pay their medical bills, that percentage increases to 29 percent for young people eighteen to twenty-four years old. The uninsured rate is almost 27 percent for those without high school diplomas (a category that includes many teen parents).

## Dim futures, dim pasts

Many studies show that when teenagers become parents, they are far more likely to lead a life limited by a shortened education, fewer personal and work opportunities, and low wages. Because of this, Americans tend to assume that unwed mothers are poor because they had their babies before finishing high school, thus reducing their chances of finding good jobs. In addition, since teen mothers are far less likely to marry and gain the additional financial support of a spouse, it may seem logical that their chances of living in poverty are high. But an increasing number of experts, looking at the data from a different angle, are framing a new question: What if poverty itself causes teen pregnancy?

A discussion of this issue appears in the book *Dubious Conceptions: The Politics of Teenage Pregnancy* by Kristin Luker, a professor of sociology, who suggests that childhood poverty is a precursor to teen pregnancy:

> A compelling body of scholarship now shows that although people who become parents as teenagers will eventually be poorer than those who do not, a very large proportion of that difference is explained by preexisting factors. Well over half of all women who give birth as teenagers come from profoundly

*Many pregnant teens come from a background of poverty.*

poor families, and more than one-fourth come from families who are slightly better off but still struggling economically. Taken together, more than 80 percent of teenage mothers were living in poverty or near-poverty long before they became pregnant.[14]

The National Campaign to Prevent Pregnancy, which has also investigated the connection between poverty and teen pregnancy, reports that "youths at greatest risk [for teen pregnancy] are more likely to live in areas with: high poverty rates, low levels of education, high residential turnover, and high divorce rates. . . . [T]heir mothers and older sisters are more likely to have given birth as adolescents."[15]

## Dropouts first

Balancing the argument that poverty and its attendant circumstances may contribute to the overall incidence of pregnancy among teens is the contention that poor educational achievement may in some cases lead to teenage pregnancy. As researchers note, there may be a connection between a girl's lack of success in school (either because she does not read or write well or for other reasons), resulting in low self-esteem, and a tendency to become pregnant as a teen.

Kristin Luker analyzes pregnancy rates among high school dropouts from a slightly different angle:

> Some estimates suggest that as many as one-fourth to one-third of teenage mothers drop out before they get pregnant. In one recent study a *majority* of the dropouts had a baby more than nine months after they left school, a fact clearly indicating that pregnancy could not have "caused" the dropping out. Other studies suggest that young women may already be drifting away from school long before pregnancy gives them an official excuse to do so.[16]

*A girl's lack of success in school can lead to feelings of inferiority, which may increase her likelihood of becoming pregnant.*

SEATS
13-25 RIGHT
1-12 LEFT

## Lost youth

Teen parents face a day-to-day struggle that even in the best circumstances can be overwhelming. Years that should be relatively carefree for a young person are instead filled with worry and daunting responsibility. In this excerpt from a poem written for a teen sexuality and pregnancy program in New York City, one teen described the situation of her friend, Michelle:

> [Poor Michelle] carries a child
> in her body at the age of sixteen.
> Poor Michelle who once was a little girl
> tells me never to do what she has done.[17]

One sixteen-year-old mother complained, "I absolutely hate hearing everyone talk about that great party on the weekend or how they are going out of town over spring break. It seems that I am missing out on my childhood years. When my daughter grows up and asks me what I did when I was a teen, all I will be able to say is 'I changed your diapers and prepared your formula.'"[18]

Helena, a seventeen-year-old interviewed by author Evelyn Lerman, had a strong message for her peers:

> Listen to me. You might think a guy is perfect, but one night isn't worth changing your whole life for. You might think you can handle it because you've taken care of a brother or a cousin. But this isn't part-time. You have to be strong. If you still want to party, you're not ready for a baby. If you don't have the money to take care of a baby, you're not ready. If you like to come home from school and just relax and not have other jobs to do, you're not ready. If you can't buy your baby what he needs, if you like to sleep a lot, if you like to not worry a lot, you're not ready.
>
> There's a long, hard road in front of us, and I'm beginning to see it more clearly. I know I can do it for us and I know I will, but I'm not going to sit here and tell you it's easy. I'm telling you it's tough, and keep that in mind when some sweet-talking guy shows up and tells you he loves you. If you're not ready to be a mother, forget it.[19]

The consequences of teen parenthood are more severe for teen mothers, but teen fathers suffer as well in comparison to men whose partners are over twenty years old when

they have children. For the younger fathers, delinquent behaviors and alcohol abuse or drug dealing often increase. Many finish fewer years of school and, as reported in 1997 by a private organization in New York that works to combat poverty, earn about three thousand dollars less per year for the eighteen years following the birth of their first child.

*The many responsibilities faced by teen parents can be overwhelming.*

## Society expresses disapproval

Young parents may feel that they are missing out on normal teenage life because they are tied down with parenting

*Teen fathers find parenthood difficult, too, although the consequences are often less daunting for them than for teen mothers.*

responsibilities. But in some cases the cause of a teen mother's lack of opportunity is, instead, based on society's disapproval of her behavior.

Seventeen-year-old Somer Chipman wanted more than anything to be initiated into her Kentucky school's chapter of the National Honor Society. But she was denied membership because she was an unwed mother. In another case, sixteen-year-old Lynn Spurlock believed she was a strong candidate for the Rose Court in Pasadena's Tournament of Roses. Like Chipman, Spurlock was excluded because of her status as unmarried teen mother.

Two editorial responses to these situations expressed conflicting attitudes about the girls' exclusion from these activities. Naomi Schaefer, then an intern on the *Wall Street Journal*'s editorial page, strongly disagreed with Chipman's exclusion from the honor society. In her view, Chipman was being punished because she took a moral stand against abortion and had her baby. "No doubt the Honor Society's officials (admirably) intend to improve the character of students by upholding standards of conduct, but their actual message is less about behavior than about appearances. It is very clear who will be rewarded by the society's policy—girls who end their pregnancies before anyone notices and boys who don't admit to fathering children."[20]

But *Los Angeles Times* writer Karen Grigsby Bates had no sympathy for Spurlock:

> Sometimes the choice we make in one instance precludes the opportunities we might have in another. The choice to become sexually active has consequences, and one of the consequences is that because the wonders and pleasures of parenthood are now open to them, the wonders and pleasures of other experiences may be closed.
>
> The Rose Bowl requirements should stay as they are. When the Rose Court floats by, little girls who fantasize about wearing the glittering tiaras should look in awe and vow to try out for Rose Queen one day. And remember, when they're older, that saying 'no' to sexual pressures of the moment might result in a 'yes' that is of more lasting importance to them later.[21]

## Babies at risk

Like their young parents, the babies of teens lead lives that are more "at risk" than the lives of babies born to older, more settled parents. "At risk" in this context refers to the likelihood that babies of teens will have health problems, get less education, and, as adults, earn less money.

Neonatal (newborn) health problems may arise because adolescent girls, in contrast to more mature women, tend to act in ways that can harm an unborn child. Poor eating habits or experimenting with drugs or alcohol—behaviors that a girl herself may outgrow without suffering long-term harmful effects—can lead to devastating, permanent harm to babies. In addition, a pregnant teen is less likely to seek or obtain good quality prenatal medical care than an older or married woman: Some teens may deny the pregnancy and others may feel uncomfortable confiding in an adult or seeing a doctor. Many simply cannot afford medical care.

Some teen mothers carry sexually transmitted diseases without knowing it, and some of those who are aware of the condition do not seek treatment. As the Centers for Disease Control and Prevention explains, babies are highly susceptible to these diseases:

> STDs can be transmitted from a pregnant woman to the fetus, newborn, or infant before, during, or after birth. Some STDs (like syphilis) cross the placenta and infect the fetus during its development. Other STDs (like gonorrhea, chlamydia, hepatitis B, and genital herpes) are transmitted from the mother to the infant as the infant passes through the birth canal. HIV infection can cross the placenta during pregnancy, infect the newborn during the birth process, and, unlike other STDs, infect an infant as a result of breast-feeding.[22]

Thirty percent of babies born to mothers with HIV will be born with HIV. A woman with syphilis has a 40 percent chance of delivering a baby that is stillborn (dead) or that dies soon after birth. Other STD complications include diseases and disabilities that may appear immediately or later in the child's life: infections; pneumonia; brain damage or motor disorders; blindness, deafness, or other organic damage; and diseases such as hepatitis, meningitis, or chronic liver disease.

The National Campaign to Prevent Teen Pregnancy reports that 28 percent more teens have low-birth-weight babies than women ages twenty to twenty-four, a condition that can cause serious problems in the baby's infancy and throughout its life. The infant mortality (death) rate is also a cause for real concern. Among teens, the rate is 50 percent higher than among women over twenty.

## The risk of poor parenting

Even if they are born healthy, the odds are stacked against the babies of parents who are themselves hardly

more than children. Good parenting takes a great deal of skill, and relatively few teens manage to develop that skill. As summarized by the National Campaign to Prevent Teen Pregnancy:

*Teen mothers may not be mature enough to provide the proper environment and sensitive nurturing that babies need.*

> Children born to teen mothers are at higher risk of poor parenting because their mothers—and often their fathers as well—are typically too young to master the demanding job of being a parent. Still growing and developing themselves, teen mothers are often unable to provide the kind of environment that infants and very young children require for optimal development. Recent research, for example, has clarified the critical importance of sensitive parenting and early cognitive stimulation for adequate brain development. Given the importance of careful nurturing and stimulation in the first three years of life, the burden [borne] by babies with parents who are too young to be in this role is especially great.[23]

From babyhood on, children of teens are less likely than children of older women to receive proper nutrition and health care. Later in life they may have more difficulty in school, repeating grades twice as often as other kids, achieving lower scores on standardized tests, and finding themselves less likely to graduate from high school but more likely to be unemployed. According to one study they are almost three times more likely to land in jail during adolescence. History often repeats itself, with the daughters of teen parents becoming teen parents themselves.

## An extreme response

Because of the strains faced by teen parents, teens are twice as likely as adults to abuse or neglect their children. And in a few rare cases, teen parents have been known to kill their babies.

In the 1990s cases involving teenagers who killed their babies took an unexpected turn. As a reporter for Knight-Ridder Newspapers wrote "[n]eonaticide [killing newborns] is no longer predominantly the act of deprived, disadvantaged, desperate girls, experts agree. Now the killer is just as likely to be affluent, educated and outwardly well-adjusted. . . ."[24]

As summarized in the article, these sad cases of infant deaths include the highly publicized story of teen parents in New Jersey who put their new baby in a trash bin behind a motel. Another troubled teen hid her new baby in a gym bag, and a girl who gave birth at her high school prom allegedly strangled the infant and threw it in the trash.

### Society's costs

While infanticide is a subject of concern, its rare occurrence makes it a less frequent topic of discussion for experts and lawmakers reviewing the problem of teen pregnancy. Instead, these adults focus on evidence that shows that teen pregnancy—a problem some see as purely personal—is, in fact, a grave problem for American society as a whole. As the Annie E. Casey Foundation (a private foundation that works to improve the lives of at-risk kids) explains: "[Teen births are] often to young women and men who lack the financial and emotional resources to care adequately for their children. And when parents are financially and emotionally unprepared, their children are more likely to be cared for either by other relatives, such as grandparents, or by taxpayers through public assistance."[25] According to data tabulated by the Centers for Disease Control and Prevention, costs to the public from teenage childbearing totaled $120 billion from 1985 to 1990.

Given the costs of teen pregnancy to young parents, their babies, and society, it is no wonder that when the subject of teen pregnancy is discussed, it is nearly always in the context of a *problem*.

# 2

# How Does It Happen?

TEEN PREGNANCY IS, of course, the result of teen sexual activity. And although the percentage of American teens having sexual intercourse dropped from 54 in 1991 to 48 in 1997, it is still far higher than the 1970 rate of 29 percent. In addition, in a July 2000 article the *Washington Post* reported that during that same time period the average age of first sexual intercourse dropped a full year—down to seventeen for girls and sixteen for boys. In the same article the *Post* also reported statistics suggesting that 20 percent of all fifteen-year-olds have had sex at least once—indicating that "even as the overall percentage of sexually active teens has declined slightly during the past couple of years—for girls under 15 it has continued to increase."[26]

## Uniquely modern problems

American teens are more aware of sex than ever before. They constantly see sexual images on television and the Internet, and in movies, video games, and the print media. Nevertheless, American teens are ill-prepared to handle their sexuality. They often lack the maturity and sense of responsibility to deal appropriately with their feelings and urges. To complicate the problem, American teens are offered little clear guidance from American adults who themselves disagree about how best to handle the behaviors that result from adolescent sexuality.

Healthy people experience hormonal changes during adolescence that lead them to eventually become sexually active. This physical change is a normal part of human growth and development. But as young Americans enter the twenty-first century, these hormonal changes are happening earlier than ever. At the same time, young men and women are marrying later than their parents and grandparents did. Since the 1950s, the age at which Americans marry

*Hormonal changes during adolescence spark sexual interest among teens.*

has risen steadily—from about twenty-three for men and twenty for women then, to a 1998 average of nearly twenty-seven for men and twenty-five for women. At the same time, the age at which boys and girls reach sexual maturity has declined dramatically, as discussed by marriage, family, and child counselor Jessica B. Gillooly:

> In the United States, children have been growing larger and maturing earlier since the beginning of the 1900s. In the past one hundred years, the average age of a girl's first menstrual cycle has decreased from approximately fourteen years to an average of twelve years. Currently some girls as young as nine or ten begin their normal menstrual cycle. Even though boys do not have such an outward sign of sexual maturity as menstruation, it is reasonable to assume that boys are also reaching their sexual maturity earlier than previous generations. . . .
>
> No one is absolutely certain why children are maturing younger. The most accepted theory is that improved health care has increased children's weight and speeded up their growth rate. Prenatal and postnatal vitamins, enriched foods such as milk and bread, and overall improved nutrition and health care contribute to increased body weight. [Inherited characteristics] also play a part in the onset of adolescence.[27]

## Risky business

Because of the emotional stresses and physical consequences (STDs and pregnancy) associated with sex, most adults see it as a behavior best left to adults—ideally, married adults. However, with statistically more than a decade between the onset of sexual maturity and marriage, many teens have a difficult time managing their sexual urges. Their situation is made more difficult by virtue of the fact that they are teens—a group that tends not to fully realize the consequences of their actions and may not therefore take responsibility for birth control if they do engage in sex.

In addition, adolescents are struggling to define themselves and, in the process, may engage in activities such as drinking or taking drugs that can lessen willpower and lead to unwanted and later regretted sexual contact. These contacts are also more likely to lead to pregnancy. As reported by the National Campaign to Prevent Teen Pregnancy, "Teens

using drugs and alcohol are more likely to put themselves in sexually risky situations and are much less likely to use contraception."[28]

Using drugs or alcohol in a setting that could lead a teen to have sex with a stranger is especially unwise, because of the risk of contracting HIV or other STD. As Beatrice Sparks explains in her comments to the diary, *It Happened to Nancy*, "It is . . . risky to combine drinking or drug use with sex, because alcohol and drugs impair your reactions and long-range reasoning abilities, and you might possibly lose your head and forget or momentarily not care."[29]

*Alcohol and drugs can cloud judgment when it comes to sex.*

## Sex is great! Sex can be fatal!

In an ideal world, teens would always know how to respond to natural sexual urges in ways appropriate to their age and family environment. However, instead of receiving clear guidance from society as a whole, teens often receive conflicting messages. *Washington Post* reporter Liza Mundy speculates on the challenges for teens today:

> I've wondered what it must be like, for girls, and for boys, too, to be coming of age in an era shaped by both the 60s sexual revolution and the 80s AIDS onslaught; coming of age in the time of "Dawson's Creek" and "Sex in the City"; a time of HIV and Eminem; a time when Lorena and John Bobbitt and Monica Lewinsky and Bill Clinton have done more than anybody else to insinuate terms like "penis" and "oral sex" into family newspapers like this one. A time when the media—all media, even mainstream media—are more sexualized than they've ever been, and yet, at the same time, the consequences of sex are depicted so grimly, by cultural conservatives and liberals alike. What does it feel like—how does a kid respond—when the messages are so mixed and so insistent?
>
> Sex is great!
>
> Sex can be fatal![30]

The National Campaign to Prevent Teen Pregnancy reports similar concerns, stating that American teens "live in a culture that sends them mixed and often destructive messages about sexuality, relationships, and developing a mature identity. Even the most advantaged teen faces pressure to make unwise and unhealthy decisions about sex."[31]

Other observers agree that confusion about sexual roles leads boys and girls to make sexual decisions they may later regret—from having sex at all, to failing to use birth control.

## A search for manhood

Teenage boys define their sense of self through media images and by observing adult men and peers, input that often equates masculinity with having sex. Thus, boys may forget—as a teen fatherhood program described by *Los Angeles Times* reporter Sarah Yang emphasizes—that "the original definition of machismo, [is] of being a man who takes care of his family both emotionally and economically."[32] One program participant reflected on his attitude at age thirteen, telling Yang that for him and his peers being a "man" had meant going after girls for sex.

Although in many cases boys express and pursue satisfaction of sexual urges more openly than girls, boys do not always feel free to make their own choices. As seventeen-year-old Nick said in a *Newsweek* roundtable, "I did feel pressure—from everything around me. Friends, media, everything. It was almost like afterwards it was almost a relief—I did it, it's over, good. I'm not a virgin anymore. I've done it, there's no anxiety about having sex anymore."[33]

## Girls struggle

For girls the situation is especially confusing. Planned Parenthood consultant Anna Runkle tries to bridge the gap between herself, a mature adult, and perplexed teens by using "we" and "us" in discussing an uncomfortable phase many girls experience:

> It is fairly common for us to have confusion or mixed feelings about sex. We live in a culture that has no clear definition of healthy sexuality, a fact that strongly affects women, and young women in particular. Many of us grew up with mixed messages that gave us the feeling that if we weren't having sex we were somehow losers. Yet if we were having sex, some people considered us bad or "slutty." This confusion was a factor that led many of us to have unprotected sex. Many of us thought that using birth control made us look like we were "expecting" sex.[34]

Girls report having sex for reasons they later find inadequate. One student, expressing regret about having had sex while she was a middle-school student, said, "I was just trying to please [my boyfriend]."[35] Another girl admitted that she put her boyfriend's desires ahead of her own concerns about safe sex: "If I ask him to use a condom, he won't feel like a man."[36]

## 700 times no

The dilemma for girls was documented by Liza Mundy in her *Washington Post* article. The reporter visited a middle school in an affluent suburb of Washington, D.C., where she asked an eighth-grade girl to describe her typical contacts with boys. The girl described how two boys asked nearly every day when she was going to give them oral sex.

*Girls face pressure from boys to have sex, and many do in order to gain acceptance or to satisfy their own curiosity.*

"They always ask," she says. "Even if you say no 700 times, they'll always ask you."

What if the boys were to suddenly leave her alone and stop asking? "I would think they didn't like me or something," she says, "or that the other girls are prettier or, like, better than me."

What if she gives in? Just goes ahead and gets it over with? She has thought about this [and realizes that people would find out]. She doesn't think it would affect her reputation; you only get a bad reputation if you have sex with every boy who asks you. But the one thing she knows is that if she did it, even once, and people found out, her day would be one endless stream of requests. "They would ask me, and ask me, even more than they do now."

In other words, this girl . . . is making complex moral calculations all day long, measuring popularity, fending off unwanted commentary, admitting to curiosity, assessing risk.[37]

## Wanting babies

While some teens have sex because they feel pressured or confused, or cannot resist giving in to natural physical urges, others view sex as a means to an end. Many girls have a difficult time analyzing their motives for having sex without using any contraceptive measures. But some experts estimate that as many as 15 percent of teen pregnancies are intended. Teens who become pregnant on purpose may lack self-esteem. They may see pregnancy as a way to fit in with peers or stay close to the father. Some believe that becoming a mother will allow them to escape an unpleasant situation at home, or to otherwise achieve what is, in their minds, a better life.

In fact, some teen mothers do describe their lives as improved. Eighteen-year-old Dena said, "Until I got pregnant I didn't care at all, but once I knew I was going to be a mother, I began to study, to take care of myself, to eat right, and to work hard. It worked for me because now I'm doing well with [my son], school, and work."[38]

Another eighteen-year-old, Shanika, confided:

> Something happened to me when I got pregnant, something that surprised me. It was a feeling even stronger than my negative image of myself and the negative reinforcements of my parents. Here was a baby going to be born! Here was a reality check! I was going to have to be a mom myself. . . .

> My grades went from C's and D's to A's and B's, and my lifestyle changed completely. I was lucky enough to become part of a program for teenage mothers in which I had day care, alternative high school education, parenting training, and two marvelous women who went to work on my self-esteem with a vengeance. They succeeded in doing a lot with it, and I don't know how to thank them adequately for all their work and care.[39]

Another study documented the pride of a girl named Catherine, who believed that becoming a mother had been her salvation. "If I didn't get pregnant I would have continued on a downward path, going nowhere. They say teenage pregnancy is bad for you, but it was good for me. I know I can't mess around now, I got to worry about what's good for [my two-year-old daughter] and for me."[40]

## Rites of passage

Research conducted in Washington, D.C., suggests that one reason disadvantaged teens deliberately start families is a belief that becoming a parent will help them establish a place in society. *Washington Post* reporter Leon Dash discovered examples of this pattern in a poor area of the city.

> I found that the girls, far from being passive victims, were often equal—or greater—actors than their boyfriends in exploring sexuality and becoming pregnant. The girls were as often the leaders in their desire to have a child as the boys were. I

*Some teens believe that having a child will solve their problems.*

did not find one adolescent couple where both partners were ignorant about the results of sexual activity without the use of contraception.

In time it became clear that for many girls in the poverty-stricken community of Washington Highlands, a baby is a *tangible* achievement in an otherwise dreary and empty future. It is one way of announcing: I *am* a woman. For many boys in Washington Highlands, the birth of a baby represents an identical rite of passage. The boy is saying: I *am* a man.[41]

*In some cases both girls and boys consider the birth of a baby a rite of passage into adulthood.*

In the book *For Real: The Uncensored Truth About America's Teenagers*, authors Jane Pratt and Kelli Pryor discovered that pregnancy is a rite of passage for some teens who are not disadvantaged. "In Akron, Ohio, which has one of the highest teen pregnancy rates in the country, Misha [a girl] tells me, 'Every girl's goal is to be pregnant by fifteen. It's like life's a party, and it's her initiation to the party. If you don't, you're out of it. . . . A lot of girls get abortions, too. It's just getting pregnant that's the thing. So you can say you did. You don't have to have the baby.'"[42]

In California, pregnancies among gang members are sometimes seen as a way of insuring a legacy. A *Los Angeles Times* reporter interviewed John Williams, a program officer for the California Community Foundation. Williams theorized, "Many of these people don't think they'll live a long time, so having a child is their way of expressing themselves, of proving they have relevance."[43] One former gang member expressed his feelings about purposely becoming a father with his girlfriend. "There was an emptiness inside of me, and I thought if I have a baby, I could give him everything I couldn't have."[44]

## Girls and men

Similar emotions may make younger teenage girls vulnerable to older men who inappropriately seek sexual relationships with inexperienced girls. These men, who often show little concern for the mental and physical well-being of their young partners, may deliberately seek out girls with low self-esteem, or who crave male approval or attention. Commentators, reviewing statistics that show that young teenage girls often become pregnant with these significantly older teenage boys or men (in many cases, the youngest girls with the older males), express concern about what they characterize as predatory behavior by these older men.

Recent studies suggest that there is good reason for worry; researchers now report that the very youngest teen girls often engage in sex without wanting to. Reviewing 1995 statistics that indicate that 19 percent of girls younger than fifteen have had sex (up from 11 percent in 1988), *Washington Post* reporter Mundy wrote:

> Sex at this age is also less likely to be consensual and more likely to be coercive, though pressure to have sex often

comes from boys in their own age group, it also frequently comes from older boys, and many young girls who do have sex do so with boys who are several years older. According to one study, 24 percent of girls who had sex at age 14 or under reported that it was "nonvoluntary"—basically, rape or molestation.[45]

Journalist Oliver Starr Jr. declared:

The exploitation of teenage girls by older men may be one of the nation's most serious social problems, but it seldom is written or talked about. . . . [A] 1992 California Department of Health Services study showed that more than three-quarters of these children were fathered by men older than 20 and more than 70 percent of the births were out of wedlock. The study further found that men older than 20 also father five times more births among junior-high-school girls than do junior-high-school boys.

For girls in junior high, the father is on average 6.5 years older. When the mother is 12 years old or younger, the father averages 22.[46]

One expert cited by Starr, Joe S. McIlhaney, a gynecologist who specializes in STDs, offers the following interpretation of these statistics: "'These studies highlight the problem that a substantial portion of teenage sexual activity is more a matter of manipulation, coercion or abuse than anything else.'"[47]

In a literature-based teen sexuality program in New York City, two eighth-grade girls, knowing the risks of their own relationships with older boys or men, counseled fifth- and sixth-grade girls:

Jasmine: When you go out with a guy, you can't really trust him so much because they can tell you are all virgins . . . they try to sweet talk you. You can't really believe that because they try to sweet talk you . . . and you won't know this. . . .

Sandra: And you should always watch out for the older guys. Stay with your own age group.[48]

## Women too soon

Some commentators believe the media plays a big role in sexualizing young girls. In a 2000 article, Brian Lowry, a *Los Angeles Times* television critic, focused on television shows aimed at teenagers whose stars were being promoted through sexually suggestive photos in magazines popular with grown men. Among shows on the WB Network, he found that most of the lead actresses

> are in their 20s but play high school students on shows wildly popular among teenage girls; . . . It's easy to wonder, then, about what message girls take away from their weekly exposure to the likes of [21-year-old 'Roswell' star Katherine] Heigl, 'Dawson Creek's' Katie Holmes (22), 'Angel's' Charisma Carpenter (26 when introduced as a teen on 'Buffy the Vampire Slayer') or Leslie Bibb, the 25-year-old star of 'Popular.' Are 14 and 15-year-old females out there thinking they should look good enough to model lingerie in a magazine aimed at [grown men]?[49]

*Katie Holmes, star of* Dawson's Creek. *Television shows popular with teens frequently depict sexual situations.*

In the words of one nineteen-year-old who participated in a *Newsweek* and *Seventeen* magazine roundtable about sex, girls' role models lead them to think they should be sexy earlier and earlier.

> I don't recall having sexuality pushed in my face when I was 10 or 11. But I have a younger half-sister who is 11 years old, and she's a very big fan of Britney Spears and the Spice Girls, and she tries to emulate them in the way she dresses and the way she acts . . . I see her wanting to wear clothes that I would never have considered wearing. I don't remember going through that at her age.[50]

## Is it love?

Peer pressure also plays a significant role in teens' sexual behavior. A Tennessee woman, Cathi Woods, took an informal survey in an attempt to determine what causes teens to have sex. Reporter Gary Thomas describes this research, which Woods cited to promote her view that encouraging teens to abstain from sex would help prevent teen pregnancy:

> Woods polled hundreds of sixth to ninth graders, asking them why they were hav-

ing sex. . . . [O]nly one student answered "because I'm in love." Seventy-nine percent said they engaged in premarital sexual relations to "fit in or be cool." The second most-popular answer—among males, not females—was "because it feels good." (Interestingly, not a single female chose this answer.)[51]

*Girls as young as ten or eleven want to dress like teen idol Britney Spears, whose wardrobe is sexually provocative.*

One girl quoted in Thomas's article suggested that teens see sex as inevitable. "[T]hey feel like they don't have any other choice. If they want to stay with whoever they're with, they have to go on to another level."[52]

But other commentators believe that adults should not discount the powerful emotional attachments that can arise between teen boys and girls. Often trivialized by the expression "puppy love," romantic feelings between teens can be stronger than many adults realize. And, since numerous aspects of the culture support the view that sex is the best expression of feelings between males and females, many teen couples have sex without carefully considering the risk of pregnancy or other consequences.

# 3

# Coming to Terms with Parenthood

LEARNING THAT SHE is pregnant is a powerful and disconcerting experience for a teen. Because the truth can be so frightening, a girl who notices that her menstrual period is late may for a time fail to acknowledge the significance of this symptom. But pregnancy will not go away with wishful thinking. Pregnant teens must eventually grapple with what is happening to them, but medical and social experts suggest that early acceptance of the new reality is preferable to prolonged denial. They reason that if a girl does not confront the reality of her pregnancy in its earliest months, she could, by inaction, be constrained to carry an unwanted pregnancy to term.

Early acknowledgment of pregnancy is considered equally important for a girl who intends to give birth because she can then begin the medical care and healthy lifestyle habits that will benefit her and her baby. In addition, if the pregnant teen is considering placing her baby with adoptive parents, she will need time to explore different types of adoption and to initiate legal proceedings.

Finally, a teen who decides to keep her baby will need time to make decisions and plans. How will she support a child? Can she still manage school? Should she get married? What if she just lives with the baby's father? These tough options will be considered while the girl is undergoing dramatic physical and emotional changes.

## Facing facts

Although a small number of girls manage to avoid admitting they are pregnant until well into the pregnancy (in rare cases, until they actually give birth), most sexually active girls recognize that a late menstrual period is a serious (though not sure) sign of pregnancy. Home pregnancy tests sold in drugstores may be used by girls who want to confirm their status inexpensively and privately. However, medical practitioners caution that unless these tests are used properly, the results may be confusing or inaccurate.

Because of this potential for confusion, health care professionals generally favor a more formal approach to confirming pregnancy—with a visit to a physician or public or private family planning clinic. There, a urine test and physical exam are performed to definitively determine pregnancy. These professionals see another benefit in consulting a doctor at this early stage: If the girl is not pregnant but intends to remain sexually active, and is not using an effective form of birth control, she may receive advice about birth control and a prescription appropriate for her situation. If the girl is pregnant she may begin her prenatal (pregnancy) care, which is essential to protect the health of the mother and baby.

Prenatal medical visits will continue until the baby is born, occurring once a month at first, then about every two weeks late in the pregnancy, and once a week the month before the due date. In addition to monitoring the growth of the unborn baby (the fetus) by measuring the girl's abdomen, checking for adequate (or excessive) weight gain by the mother, and listening to the heartbeat of the fetus, the doctor or health care practitioner will take the mother's blood pressure.

Monitoring blood pressure is an important part of the prenatal exam; high blood pressure coupled with other symptoms can be a sign of preeclampsia, a condition that can cause labor to occur before the fetus is mature enough to survive. One expert describes the potentially serious results of this condition: "In its most severe form preeclamp-

sia becomes eclampsia, and it can seriously affect [the mother] as well as the baby, causing convulsions and possibly even a state of coma [in the mother]. The following symptoms can all be signs of eclampsia: headache, flashing lights, nausea, vomiting, and pain in the abdomen."[53]

*Responsible pregnant teens make regular visits to a health care professional for prenatal checkups.*

## Following a proper diet

In addition to monitoring the health of the mother-to-be, the medical practitioner will discuss her lifestyle. Doctors generally advise pregnant patients to eat a balanced diet with enough protein and calcium, and to avoid "junk food." To supplement an expectant mother's diet, doctors may also prescribe daily prenatal vitamins. However, the doctor will also warn that while these supplements are recommended, other legal medicines—prescription or over-the-counter—can be harmful to the baby and should not be taken without medical approval.

For girls and young women who have prided themselves on being thin, a waistline that is growing seemingly out of control can be distressing. This concern was expressed at a childbirth class in California by one young mother-to-be who asked how she could keep her stomach flat during pregnancy. Of course, the answer is that she cannot, and that attempting to do so by restricting caloric intake during pregnancy can be dangerous for the mother and the fetus.

A doctor's concern about a pregnant patient's diet is based on research that shows that the diet of the mother-to-be can affect her baby's development. As authors Dr. William Sears and Martha Sears explain in *The Pregnancy Book:*

> Studies show that the better a pregnant woman's nutrition, the more likely she is to deliver a healthy baby. Eating too little (or too little of the needed foods) increases the risk of giving birth to a baby who may be born too soon or too small, have birth defects, or have breathing and blood chemistry problems at birth. Poor prenatal nutrition increases the risk of problems ranging from stillbirth to developmental delay.[54]

The risks associated with too-small babies is further explained by the National Campaign to Prevent Teen Pregnancy: "Low birth weight raises the probabilities of infant death, blindness, deafness, chronic respiratory problems, mental retardation, mental illness, and cerebral palsy. In addition, low birth weight doubles the chances that a child will later be diagnosed as having dyslexia, hyperactivity, or another disability."[55]

## Dangers of smoking and drinking alcohol

Low birth weight is also one of several serious problems that may result from smoking, drinking alcohol, or taking illegal drugs during pregnancy. Smoke from an expectant mother's cigarette or from "secondhand" sources reduces the flow of blood and oxygen to the fetus, interfering with normal growth and development. In addition, chemicals in cigarette smoke may harm the brain of the developing fetus. Studies show that as a result, "[c]hildren of mothers who smoked during pregnancy, especially those of mothers who smoked more than one pack a day . . . have . . . decreased mental performance scores at age one year, reduced IQs, more behavior problems, and diminished academic performance scores in school. . . ."[56]

Just as the growing fetus in effect "smokes" when the mother smokes, the fetus "drinks" when the mother drinks alcohol. And since it is not known if even minor amounts of alcohol can harm the fetus, many experts, including the U.S. surgeon general, strongly recommend that expectant mothers drink no alcohol. Excessive alcohol consumption is, however, known to cause fetal alcohol syndrome (FAS) in babies. The seriousness of this condition is summarized by Dr. William Sears and Martha Sears in *The Pregnancy Book:*

> FAS babies weigh less, are shorter, and have smaller brains than normal babies. Sometimes their brains are malformed, and they may suffer from mental retardation. Babies born with fetal alcohol syndrome have unusual facial characteristics: their eyes appear smaller than usual, their nose is short, and their upper lip is thin. They may also have abnormalities of the hands, feet, and heart.[57]

## Why say no to drugs

As bad as alcohol and tobacco can be for the health of an unborn baby, illegal drugs may well be worse. Use during pregnancy of cocaine, heroin and other narcotics, PCP (angel dust), or LSD (acid) has been linked to preterm birth, fetal death, fetal addiction, and low birth weight. Babies exposed to drugs while fetuses may grow slowly, have brain injury, exhibit irritability and fussiness, experience behavior problems, and have trouble thinking clearly. The effects of marijuana smoking are less well known, but studies suggest that the drug can cause harm, including depriving the fetus of oxygen.

Antidrug groups and the media have publicized the tragic effects on babies of mothers' drug use, and such efforts appear to be bearing fruit. Pediatricians at Brown University in Rhode Island found that being pregnant motivates many teens to stop smoking, drinking, or using marijuana, either on their own or through counseling or support programs.

## The role of teens' parents

Even girls who are not wrestling with the difficult problems associated with alcohol or drug use will need help and support during pregnancy. While there were exceptions, in 2001 state laws generally allowed a teen to obtain preg-

*All pregnant teens need help and support during this stressful and often lonely period.*

nancy testing, birth control, and prenatal care without a parent's consent. However, experts agree that, in most cases, it is best for a girl to face her pregnancy with the knowledge and support of at least one parent. In fact, if she chooses to have an abortion, she may need their consent. But beyond this legal reason, parents are often in the best position to help a girl make, then follow through on, a decision about her pregnancy. Many teens, however, are reluctant or unwilling to discuss this painful situation at home. Some turn to their peers; others look for outside counseling—through school, church, or a family planning clinic.

Telling parents about a possible or actual pregnancy is never easy for an unmarried teen. Boys and girls alike may have a realistic fear of provoking expressions of disappointment and anger. While most parents are, in time, more supportive than most teens expect, nearly all parents react emotionally at first. Anticipating such a reaction, one pregnant teen asked her aunt to break the news to her mother. However, that strategy did not isolate her from her family's initial anger.

> My mom got furious. All my sisters were mad at me already. . . . My mom . . . started screaming at me. "Why did you do that?" She had trusted me. I knew I was wrong in getting pregnant, but I couldn't tell her anything because she was already so mad at me. Everybody was angry, and nobody talked to me. . . . I only saw my parents once or twice during [my pregnancy].

While this girl's parents were not supportive at first, in time the situation improved. "They didn't really want to see me [when I was pregnant], but I came back home in June. It's working pretty well."[58]

## Being pregnant

While family reaction adds considerably to the stress of teen pregnancy, even married, adult women experience emotional ups and downs during pregnancy. Some women report feeling especially happy and healthy, often in the middle three months (middle trimester). But most women also experience some discomfort and emotional turmoil as their hormonal balance shifts and the baby grows larger. For teens who are not happy about being pregnant, or whose parents or boyfriends are angry or unsupportive, the typical mood swings of pregnancy can be especially difficult.

Early in the pregnancy, expectant mothers may experience food cravings, exhaustion, and morning sickness (a queasy feeling or vomiting that usually occurs when the girls wakes up but may happen anytime during the day). Health care providers may suggest napping and taking walks to relieve exhaustion, and eating small, well-balanced meals and nibbling on saltine crackers to relieve nausea.

As her body adjusts to hormonal changes, a girl generally becomes more comfortable. The second trimester is also the time when the expectant mother feels the fetus move for the first time. For many, this event makes the pregnancy seem more real. This increased sense of connection with the unborn baby may bring joy to the mother-to-be. However, an unmarried teen who is worried about her future and the future of her baby may be distressed by the increasing reality of her situation.

While the discomforts of early pregnancy are caused mostly by hormonal changes, it is fetal growth that causes discomfort in the last months of pregnancy. As the fetus grows to fill the enlarging uterus, the mother-to-be may be unable to eat more than a few bites at a time. She may be constantly running to the bathroom. These uncomfortable sensations are a result of the increasingly larger fetus putting pressure on the bladder and stomach.

As the expectant mother carries more and more weight in the front of her body, her back may also begin to ache, a symptom women have traditionally relieved by putting their feet up. In addition, many health care providers suggest walking as a safe, comfortable way to relieve back pain and maintain overall health.

## Staying in school, seeking support

Experts on adolescents and children suggest that staying in school is one of the most important things a pregnant girl can do for herself and for her baby. Educational options vary from community to community, but all public schools are required by law to allow a pregnant student to continue with her regular program if she wants to. However, pregnant girls may benefit from the companionship and skill-building offered in programs designed especially for them. Special educational opportunities for pregnant

*Many schools and community organizations offer specialized classes for pregnant teens, who may also continue in regular programs.*

teens range from alternative schools to programs conducted within the school or at off-campus locations such as churches or YMCAs. Pregnant students may attend basic classes with other students, and then take additional classes that teach workforce and parenting skills. Counselors, social workers, and health care providers may also work with pregnant teens. Child care is offered at some schools.

For a few girls, attending school at all seems impossible during pregnancy. In this situation, school counselors can set up home tutoring. Some girls also earn a high school equivalency credential by studying for and passing a General Educational Development (GED) exam.

Coping with impending parenthood is a lot easier for girls who have the support of others, according to psychological experts. This support may be as informal as talking with trusted family members, friends, counselors, teachers, or social workers. Some girls join teen parenting groups or take parenting classes. Also, it is usual for medical providers to suggest childbirth preparation classes in which qualified instructors explain not only what will happen during the labor and delivery but also how to minimize discomfort and risk.

## The father's role

The father of the baby may feel scared, too. But how he reacts—the amount of support and commitment he is able to show at this time—will affect how the mother of the baby feels about her pregnancy. As one author put it:

> If your girlfriend is pregnant, you will certainly have opinions about what your partner should do. In most states you have no legal right to a say in whether she goes ahead with the pregnancy or not. However, this doesn't mean you should be excluded from discussions. Your attitude and support will count for a lot in helping your partner to make up her mind. Fathers have rights once the baby is born, and with those rights come all the many responsibilities of having a family.[59]

Although many boys walk away from their partners when they become pregnant, some are active fathers, ei-

ther living with or marrying the baby's mother, or continuing to be involved in other ways. One young father expressed his desire to be an active, responsible father, and advised other young fathers on how to do the same:

*Teen mothers converse at a childcare center located in their school.*

> I'm trying to change the stereotypes of teenage fathers. It's like all fathers were never there. I feel my child didn't ask to be born. My child deserves a mother and a father, and the mother and father should be equal.
>
> I feel like if I laid down with her to make the baby, I should be there. I want to be there 100 percent for my child. . . . I grew up with just my mom, and I don't want it to be like that.
>
> Spend time with your kid even if you don't have a dime in your pocket. Be there for your kid. Hug him. That's more important than anything.[60]

Researchers have identified certain characteristics that may contribute to a boy's success as a father. Those

*A teen boy with a strong attachment to his partner and their child may become an excellent parent, particularly if his own father was a good role model.*

characteristics include: a continuing friendship with and respect for his partner; a longer term relationship with that partner; having a father who was himself a good role model; and having a fierce devotion to his child.

## Making plans

While it was once assumed that unmarried teens expecting a child would get married, this is no longer the case. Most commentators point to shifts in American attitudes about unwed motherhood as a cause of the dramatic decrease in marriage as a response to teen pregnancy. As author Elinor B. Rosenberg summarizes, "Prior to the sexual revolution of the 1960s premarital sex and the babies that resulted were generally considered shameful. . . . Most birth mothers felt they had no options besides a 'shotgun wedding' or the stigma of raising the child as an unmarried mother. . . ."[61]

At the end of the twentieth century the notion that a father would wield a shotgun to "persuade" a man to marry his pregnant daughter was strange indeed. Parents no longer insisted on marriage for a daughter or son about to become a teen parent. Teens felt freer to choose what to do and rarely saw marriage as the best course of action. In fact, researchers found that in many cases the reluctance to marry resulted from a moral view that it is wrong to undertake a marital commitment unless the partners feel sure it will last. Instead, couples who want to stay together at least for a time will live together without being married— either with parents, other family members, or on their own.

Each living arrangement has its challenges. Living in an extended family arrangement may cause stress if the teens resent what they see as interference from the grandparents who, in turn, may feel overburdened with child care and other duties. A teen father living with his girlfriend's (or wife's) parents may feel as if he has lost control of his life or new family. And if the grandparents continually blame him for the pregnancy, he is likely to feel unwelcome as well.

Authors Jeanne Warren Lindsay and Sharon Githens Enright, who have worked with teen parents, describe the problems that may result from extended family living situations:

> Many custodial teen parents continue to live with their parent(s) for at least two years after their babies are born. Therefore, much teen parenting is done in the context of the family system. . . .
>
> Often there is a honeymoon effect for a couple of months after the baby is born. The family adores the baby, and everything may go well for [a while]. Soon, however, the newness wears off, and the routine is there. The young mother no longer gets the attention; now it goes to the baby. The grandparents dote on the baby and the young mother is out in left field.
>
> At this point, the teenager may pull away emotionally. She may go see her friends and leave the baby with the grandparents. Being parented by the grandparents may seem safe for the baby at this point, but it can cause a lot of problems [because it raises the question,] Who is the 'real' parent?[62]

## On their own

While living with parents can be challenging, living alone can be overwhelming for a single mother or a teen couple trying to finish school. Babies need to be fed, changed, and comforted around the clock. New parents will find themselves losing sleep and struggling to keep up with the shopping and laundry. They may be frustrated when their baby cries because they cannot always tell what the baby needs. While they may have school or community day care available to them, many must place their babies at a licensed in-home or independent facility. Finding high quality care from such providers is one problem; affording it is likely to be another.

In *Teenage Fathers*, authors Karen Gravelle and Leslie Peterson quote a new father who felt consumed by the day-to-day responsibilities:

*A teen mother living alone with her child may be overwhelmed by the challenges she faces.*

"*Pampers.* Pampers here. Pampers there, constantly saving money so we could have this, have that." Dealing with his little daughter wasn't easy either. "When my daughter was sick, running her to the hospital. Being able to be patient . . . you know, a lot of things. Especially when it's a newborn!" Wayne exclaims.

"The first year was running around shopping, making sure I got the right clothes . . . she'd grow out of clothes so quick. I had to learn a lot of things like that, keeping up with her sizes. Taking her on family visits," he adds. "Everywhere I went she was like a prize fish!"[63]

*It is not unusual for a teen mother to raise her baby without a partner.*

Statistics show that girls often find themselves without a partner when they become pregnant. Although a girl may want to live on her own in order to receive government financial assistance, she must live in an adult-supervised situation. Planned Parenthood consultant Anna Runkle explained in her 1998 book what is available to and required of teens under welfare laws:

Welfare, food stamps, and Medicaid will cover medical and some living expenses for teens and their children for a lifetime total of five years. . . . [Under "Temporary Assistance to Needy Families" or TANF laws], teen mothers must live with their parents or in approved, adult-supervised situations and they must go to high school until they turn eighteen or graduate. All mothers who receive welfare must start working and at least partially support themselves within two years.[64]

Although teen motherhood is a major challenge, girls can, and do, manage. According to Runkle, "Many teen mothers say that having a baby was the best thing that ever happened to them. These mothers are comfortable with the hard work required and with the limitations on their social life. Some say having a baby gave them a focus and helped them get their lives together."[65]

# 4

# Adoption and Abortion

MANY PREGNANT TEENS decide, for any number of reasons, that parenting is not for them. Some worry that motherhood would interfere with plans for the future. Others wonder how they would cope with the day-to-day stresses of parenting, or how they would pay for a baby's needs. Some lack support from their parents or the baby's father.

Girls who decide against parenting have two other options: abortion and adoption. Far more girls choose abortion over adoption, but as with parenting, the selection of either course of action requires careful consideration of the values, circumstances, and feelings of each individual. Experts suggest that it is preferable for a girl to involve her family as she makes her way through the decision process.

## Abortion and the Supreme Court

Abortion is the termination of a pregnancy by surgically removing the fetus or embryo and the placenta from the mother's womb or by using drugs to induce the expulsion of the embryo. Abortion has been legal in all states since 1973 when the U.S. Supreme Court ruled, in the case of *Roe v. Wade*, that states could not prohibit abortions in the early months of pregnancy when the fetus is not mature enough to live outside the mother's womb. After *Roe*, the Supreme Court decided other cases—and lawmakers passed laws—that affected certain aspects of the abortion process.

*A teen's discovery that she is pregnant leads to difficult decisions.*

Based on these post-*Roe* developments, many states limit public funding for abortions or impose waiting periods on women and girls seeking abortions.

An additional development affects only girls (generally under age eighteen). In 2001 about half the states enforced laws requiring pre-abortion consent of, or notice to, one or both of a girl's parents. If a teen prefers to avoid these processes, states provide a system called "judicial bypass."

As one journalist explained, "Judicial bypass is an alternative that permits a [local] judge to determine in a courtroom hearing if a young woman is mature enough, or if it would be in her best interests, to obtain an abortion without telling her parents."[66]

Supporters of parental consent laws assert that they allow parents to be involved in the medical decisions of their daughters. However, some commentators and teens worry that the laws create emotional stress for girls and, in the worst cases, lead them to seek illegal abortions, which can cause serious medical complications or death.

In 1999 at a conference sponsored by the Center for Reproductive Law and Policy (an advocacy group that supports the right to choose abortion), Jamie Sabino, an attorney who guides minor girls through the Massachusetts judicial bypass process, summarized her clients' experiences. Reporter Ann Farmer described Sabino's discussion this way:

> First of all, [Sabino explained,] a teenager is often late in discovering she's pregnant. Then she must find the courage to arrange a court date. She must find an excuse to get out of school since Massachusetts courts are only open during school hours, and hope that the school doesn't report her absence to her parents. She must find a ride to court or hitchhike. She may feel compelled to go out of state for an abortion to avoid the system altogether.

> "With all this going on, there is at least a week or two delay engendered by the system," says Sabino, who adds that most young women are traumatized by the thought of going before a judge to discuss such an intimate matter. "Girls tell me it gives them nightmares and makes them nauseous. What may be the most important decision of their lives is being made by a stranger."[67]

## Abortion procedures

In a surgical abortion a doctor removes the embryo or fetus and placenta from the mother's womb. The procedures are less complicated in the earliest stages of the pregnancy. During the first trimester the contents of the uterus can be sucked or scraped out in about ten minutes.

Local anesthesia numbs the area of the vagina and cervix but the patient remains conscious.

Second trimester abortions, performed under local anesthesia and sedation, may be either by "dilation and evacuation" or, less commonly, by "induced abortion." A dilation and evacuation is done in two stages. In the first a procedure is performed to cause the cervix to dilate overnight. The next day a physician uses vacuum-type equipment to remove the contents of the uterus. This part of the procedure usually takes less than half an hour.

A hospital stay is required for an induced abortion. In this procedure the doctor injects a salt or hormone solution into the uterus to induce contractions. These contractions expel the fetus. The uterus may then be scraped to make sure no tissue is left.

The Alan Guttmacher Institute, a special affiliate of Planned Parenthood that conducts nonpartisan research, reports that abortions performed by competent abortion providers are generally safe, with less than 1 percent of the procedures resulting in serious medical problems. First trimester abortions are safer than second trimester abortions. In rare cases where complications do occur, they are usually signaled by heavy vaginal bleeding; fever, chills, or weakness; abdominal pain or cramping; or a vaginal discharge that smells bad.

Postabortion emotions normally range from relief to feelings of loss, guilt, and regret. Negative emotions usually pass in time. However, some girls and women, especially those who felt pressured to have the abortion or who made their decision without support from the father, parents, or friends, experience depression that requires counseling or additional medical care.

## The "abortion pill"

A combination of drugs, mifepristone and misoprostol (also called RU-486), can also be used to expel the embryo during the seven weeks following a girl's last menstrual period. If the drugs are effective, a so-called medical abortion has occurred, and no surgical procedure is required.

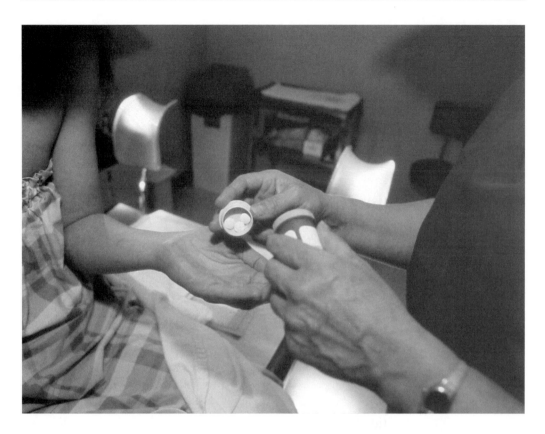

Although the process is effective more than 90 percent of the time, failure can lead to serious problems.

*A doctor dispenses the controversial "abortion pill," RU-486.*

## The rare choice of adoption

As difficult as the decision to have an abortion is for some girls, it is widely preferred over adoption as a way to handle teen pregnancy. While from 1952 to 1972 adoption was the choice of nearly one-fifth of unmarried white women, the percentage had declined to about 3 percent by 1988. By the mid-1990s less than 1 percent of *teen* unmarried mothers of all races chose adoption. Experts attribute the dramatic drop in the number of adoptions in part to the legalization of abortion after the *Roe* decision in 1973 and, in part, to the fact that by the last decades of the twentieth century single mothers were rarely stigmatized. In fact, for many girls, raising a child without a husband is more acceptable than relinquishing a baby through adoption.

## Parental pressure

A girl may feel reluctant to choose adoption because her family may disapprove of "giving away" the child. One girl described this experience to researchers during a study completed in the early 1990s: "[People] tell me I'm going to regret this the rest of my life; spend my whole life wondering where it is. But my grandparents are the worst. They say things like, 'this is our blood. How can you give up our blood relative?'"[68]

A girl who is determined to avoid this type of pressure may seek to complete the process without involving her parents. However, even though most states do not have laws requiring parents' consent, in the real world parents do become involved. As explained by the Alan Guttmacher Institute:

> In practice, it is likely that some adoption agencies and judges (all adoptions, regardless of the mother's age, have to be approved by a court) require that a young woman's parents be involved in the adoption decision. In principle, however, virtually all states consider a minor mother capable of making an independent decision about whether or not to place her child for adoption (although a few states require that the minor have a court-appointed guardian).[69]

In some instances parents exert the opposite pressure: They insist on adoption even if the teen is reluctant. This situation can cause anguish in the birth parents. In addition, some researchers believe that a girl who is pressured to give up a child through adoption may be more likely to become pregnant again.

One girl described how she felt about not making the decision on her own: "My mother convinced me that keeping the baby would ruin my life. . . . I now think she was saying that my keeping the baby would have ruined *her* life. I wish I had not let her impose her needs on me. I never really made the decision for myself."[70]

Even if a girl does not encounter resistance from her parents, she may decide against adoption because she is worried about how her child would react. As one girl told researchers, "The baby would hate me for making him go through such a thing; hate me because I wasn't there to love him."[71]

Girls may also be aware of the experience of mothers who have chosen adoption, and worry that they will suffer from the same difficult emotions. They may hear about heartache, such as that described by one teen who said, "It was definitely a traumatic experience, the hardest thing I ever did. If it hadn't been for [my counselor], I would never have made it. I learned you have to heal. You have to cry, you have to grieve. That's part of the healing process."[72]

A teen may also worry about how she will feel years later. Looking back, one woman confided, "Today, I am twenty-nine years old, I am married to a good man, I have a great job, and in every way you might think I'm a success. Still, I constantly think of my baby girl. My 'baby girl' is now a teenager."[73]

Even girls who decide to relinquish their child have difficulty at first coming to terms with their choice. One girl explained her thought processes this way, "I'd work out all these plans, but none of them ever worked. I'd be working all the time and still not have enough money, or any time to spend with my baby. I'd probably end up on welfare and it would be so hard for the baby."[74] Another girl wrestled with conflicting thoughts and emotions before deciding on adoption:

> I know that I am not ready to take good enough care of this child and that an adoptive family would give him much more emotionally, financially, and culturally. I really believe that. What I also know is that I don't want to take care of him now. . . . I want to finish school, have a career, marry . . . and live an ordinary life. . . . My heart says I'm being selfish for placing my own life goals over the hurt feelings of a child who will know I gave him away.[75]

## Independent or open adoption

Experts also suggest that teens may be reluctant to choose adoption because they are not adequately counseled on the benefits, or are not aware that "open" or "independent" adoptions allow a birth mother to be involved in the process or in her child's life. In fact, one girl expressed surprise when she learned of these other kinds of adoption. "My idea about adoption was that you throw your kid into

*Pregnant teens struggle with the difficult decision of whether to raise a baby, relinquish it through adoption, or have an abortion.*

some black hole and you never see him again."[76] This girl's notion of adoption is based on traditional closed adoption, where the baby is relinquished to a state or private agency and the birth parents and adoptive parents do not know each other's identities.

Open or independent adoptions are alternatives that might be more appealing to girls who want to choose the adoptive parents or follow the child's development. Nearly all states allow independent adoptions, where the birth mother and potential adoptive parents make contact privately, either through advertising (if allowed by state law) or by word-of-mouth. Attorneys then handle the legal details of completing the adoption, which include the birth mother's relinquishment of the baby directly to the adoptive parents she has selected.

More and more, birth parents are choosing "open" adoption, which is most often completed in the context of an independent adoption. As author Lois Gilman explains, "In open adoptions birth parents and adoptive parents meet one another, share identifying information, and communicate directly over the years. They may get together often, occasionally, or not at all as the individuals determine [initially and over time] what is best for them."[77] While open adoption allows the birth parents to participate in the child's life, the birth mother has no more rights over that child than she would in any other kind of adoption. In all types of adoption, once the legal proceedings are finalized—including approval by a court and, in some cases, consent of the father if he is found and asserts parental rights—the relinquishment is almost always permanent.

Gilman summarizes the position of those who advocate open adoption:

> For birth parents, open adoption brings a greater sense of control. While they will still grieve for their loss, they will know that they have made a place for their child and they will not be cut off from direct knowledge of their child's well-being. . . .
>
> Open adoption advocates talk about the "honesty" of this kind of adoption. . . . The unknown, say advocates, compounds [adopted] children's fears that something wrong with them must have led their birth parents to abandon them.[78]

One single mother of a three-year-old boy, who could not face having a third abortion, expressed her satisfaction with open adoption:

. . . I chose Mark and Christine to be my baby's parents. They were the first couple I called, I just knew, I had goose bumps. . . . Now I'm part of their extended family. They live in Idaho, so I went out there for Kaylie's first birthday. The trip was awesome. Christine didn't feel threatened by me. I didn't feel tense. I could be myself. I saw Kaylie standing in the airport; she had just started walking. I had tears of joy. She looks just like her birth dad.[79]

But although open adoption works for many, it is still a relatively new arrangement. Some commentators express concern about the long-term effects of open adoption on children, especially since young birth mothers, whose lives, priorities, and interests often change as they mature,

*Adoptive parents play with their children. Some unwed teens choose adoption for their babies.*

may lose interest in maintaining contact. As Kathleen Silber, coauthor of *Children of Open Adoption*, explains: "We keep seeing more and more that kids are upset. They've been used to having a certain relationship with a birth mother, even if it's just hearing from her once a year. When the child stops hearing from her for two years, the child perceives this as a rejection—'I was given up once and now she's rejected me again.'"[80]

One adoptive mother, Becky Miller, who appears on panels about open adoption, summarized her concerns about the new process of open adoption this way: "We all wonder how the kids will view the situation in ten or fifteen years. Will they think that this is strange? Whether you are the adoptive parent or the birth parent, you hope that your child understands and accepts how this all came about."[81]

## Reunions may work for some and not others

Although open adoption is becoming more common, a girl may choose traditional closed adoption because she is concerned about problems that may arise with open adoption. Even in closed adoptions, a birth mother may be able to connect with her child later in life. A few states allow birth mothers access to original birth certificates or adoption information under certain circumstances.

Many other states allow reunions in closed adoptions. About half the states maintain "mutual consent registries." In these states, if an adult adoptee and the birth parents agree, identifying information may be given to either. About half the states allow a procedure known as "search and consent," in which an adopted child can enlist the aid of an individual or agency to contact birth parents. If the birth parents agree, their identity will be revealed to the adopted child.

Nevertheless, parents who chose closed adoptions may prefer to keep the adoption closed, in many cases because they do not wish to disrupt their child's life. Women may also worry about repercussions in their own lives. As one woman explained:

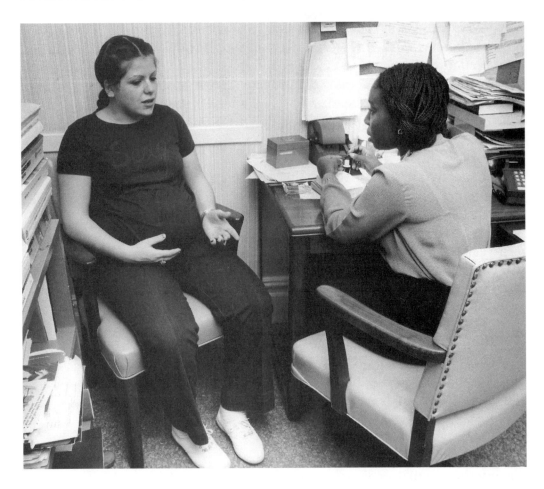

*A counselor can help a girl understand her adoption choices.*

As much as I long for him and want to see him, I know that bringing him or even the news of him into my life would destroy everything I've worked for these many years. I have a husband and other children now. None of them know. I am convinced that it would destroy my marriage and devastate my children if this child reappeared. I know that some people do have successful reunions. I just don't think it could work for me.[82]

## Finding a solution

Teens and adults alike express the notion that choosing an alternative to parenting is challenging. Neither option—abortion or adoption—is right for every pregnant teen. However, teens do, in time, face the reality of their situations and come to workable solutions to the difficult problem.

# 5

# Approaches to the Problem

AMERICAN GIRLS BECOME pregnant far more often than girls in other developed countries—twice as often as girls in England or Canada and nine times as often as girls in the Netherlands or Japan. Still, data show that teen birth rates have declined in the United States, and researchers have tried to find out why.

The Annie E. Casey Foundation summarized research on the declining birth rate:

> There are two primary reasons that teen birth rates are falling: (1) Fewer teens are having sex, and (2) more of the teens that do have sex are using contraception. . . . Researchers attribute the recent trends in teen sexual activity and contraceptive use to a variety of factors: (1) greater emphasis on delaying sexual activity; (2) more responsible attitudes among teenagers about casual sex and out-of-wedlock childbearing; (3) increased fear of sexually transmitted diseases, especially Acquired Immune Deficiency Syndrome [AIDS]; (4) the growing popularity of long-lasting contraceptive methods, such as the implant (Norplant) and the injectable (Depo-Provera) options, and possibly more consistent or correct use of other contraceptive methods; and (5) a stronger economy, with better job prospects for young people.[83]

As this complex list shows, many factors influence the behavior of teens. And because sex is a private act, it is, ultimately, the attitudes and behavior of teens rather than parents, educators, and politicians that will make the difference.

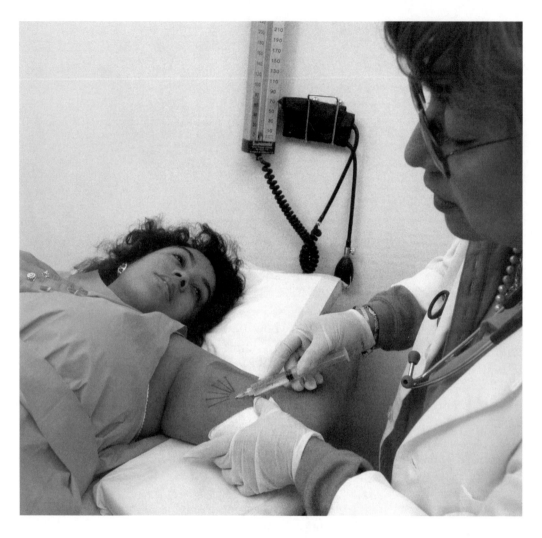

*A health practitioner inserts a contraceptive implant, one of several long-lasting contraceptive methods.*

## Two approaches to prevention

In a 1994 study conducted by Jeanne Warren Lindsay, who has written frequently about teenage pregnancy, nearly four thousand teens were asked the question, Is sex before marriage okay? More than 70 percent of the girls who were not living with a partner responded "absolutely," "probably," or "It doesn't matter." For boys the number was about 80 percent. Teens living with a partner had even fewer objections to the idea of engaging in premarital sex. Consistent with these findings, the National Campaign to Prevent Teen Pregnancy reports: "Teenagers rarely think premarital sex is immoral; rather they believe young people should abstain from sex because of the risk of getting AIDS or becoming pregnant."[84]

A majority of adults and teens support abstinence as a goal. However, most also believe that in spite of efforts to encourage abstinence, a number of teens will continue to engage in sex and that teens as a group should therefore have information about birth control. Opposing that view is a growing number of Americans who believe that teens can be taught to abstain from sex, but that the only way to effectively convey that message is through programs that teach abstinence only. By the end of the 1990s almost one-quarter of school-based programs excluded talk of birth control (except to say that it can fail) and instead focused on a strong message that kids should abstain from sex.

Supporters of abstinence-based programs see the alternative—sex education that teaches abstinence *and* birth control—as a harmful source of confusion for teens. They ask, If teens are told how to use birth control, why would they take seriously the message to abstain? They favor structuring sex education similarly to the drug education programs built around the message, "Just Say No."

States have devised slogans to get the "Just Say No" message across. Posters and billboards convey such messages as: "Avoid the pain. Abstain." "Virgin. Teach your kid it's not a dirty word." Church groups encourage teens to sign "Abstinence Pledge Cards." Celebrities like Jessica Simpson and Enrique Iglesias have also been enlisted to publicize these messages. In addition, school and community-based classes and support groups have been established.

## Preventing broken hearts

Some supporters of abstinence-only programs see them as having an emotional benefit for teens. They see abstinence as a way for boys and girls to avoid the problems that arise when they become intensely focused on each other because of a sexual relationship: jealousy, isolation from other friends, and the heartbreak that inevitably accompanies a breakup.

Kathleen Sullivan, director of an Illinois-based abstinence-only program, has observed that sexual relationships can be an emotional problem for boys as well as girls. Her views were reported in the *Christian Science Monitor:*

> [Sullivan] explains that young teenage girls are generally more mature than boys, and relationships seldom last. "The girls usually break them off and move on to older guys. These young boys hurt just as much as the girls, but they internalize it. It's shown in 'machoism,' in a defensive 'I-don't-care' attitude."[85]

## Supporting abstinence

Participation in abstinence groups may be helpful to teens who strive to abstain from sex until marriage. For example, of the ten thousand teens who participated in a study by Illinois-based "Project Reality," an abstinence group, 51 percent said they believed sexual urges could always be controlled.

*Teens demonstrate in support of sexual abstinence.*

Girls who participate in abstinence-based support groups report feeling more in control because of their participation in the group. A member of one such group, Girls Against Premarital Sex, said: "I tell my boyfriend, 'I can't have sex with you because I'm in the group.'. . . It gives me more strength to say no to my boyfriend."[86] The school nurse, Esther Splaine, who runs the group, explains why she feels girls benefit: "[I urge] girls to say, 'I'm going to take the energy I would put into a sexual relationship and channel that toward sports, grades, developing better friendships with my girlfriends.' I tell them, 'When you practice abstinence and self-control, the likelihood of getting side-tracked is so much less. The likelihood of reaching your dreams is so much greater.'"[87]

Cathi Woods, who started a successful abstinence support group in Tennessee that involved her taking late-night phone calls from teens experiencing the temptation to have sex, expressed her belief that girls ultimately benefit from abstinence. "The true empowerment of women is teaching abstinence, because abstinence gives women control of their bodies."[88]

While these commentators believe strongly in the benefits of their programs, a 2001 study suggested that, at best, abstinence programs delay rather than prevent premarital sex. In addition, the study found that teens who were taught abstinence-only, but who eventually had intercourse, were likely to do so without using birth control—increasing their risk of pregnancy or infection with a sexually transmitted disease.

## The importance of parental communication

While support for abstinence programs was increasing in the late 1990s, girls surveyed on how to prevent teen pregnancy discussed other issues. As summarized by the National Campaign to Prevent Teen Pregnancy, when girls were surveyed in 1997 about how teen pregnancy could be prevented, more than 90 percent answered, "having parents they could talk to," "having loving parents."[89]

*Open communication about sex between teens and their parents helps to reduce sexual risk-taking.*

The importance of teen-parent communication has been documented by other prevention groups. In response, programs have been developed to help increase communication between adults, especially parents, and teens. "Plain Talk," developed through the Annie E. Casey Foundation, is a neighborhood-based program initially implemented in five urban centers that uses workshops to teach parents and other adults to talk more openly and effectively with teens about how to reduce sexual risk-taking. As described by the Annie E. Casey Foundation, one Atlanta-based program, "Askable Adults"

> is a communications skills workshop designed to help adults talk to youth about puberty, dating, sex, pregnancy, health and decision-making. The eight-session workshop focuses on communication. One resident who went through the series said, "In order to deal with [youth], you have to know how to talk to them . . . we have role plays, skits [and] get different opinions about how to handle different situations."[90]

## Broader approaches

The survey published by the National Campaign to Prevent Teen Pregnancy also cited "having self respect," "being informed about sex, pregnancy and birth control," and "being aware of the responsibility of caring for a child" as important in preventing teen pregnancy.[91] In addition, it indicated other vital factors: a girl's satisfaction with her life, knowing how to use a condom, choosing the right boyfriends, and using contraceptives all the time. A little more than half of the girls also cautioned against going out with older men.

A number of programs specifically address issues on sex and dating that are important to the girls surveyed. These programs are broader in scope than abstinence-only programs. Debra Haffner, president of the Sexuality Information and Education Council of the United States, expressed the attitudes of people who support these more comprehensive sex education programs: "In the same way that we have to support the virgins in America's classrooms, we need to help young people who are sexually active."[92] While the Washington-based organization Advocates for Youth supports the notion that abstinence should be encouraged, its vice president, Debra Hauser, told the *Christian Science Monitor*, "We also believe strongly in providing information about contraception. The majority of people will eventually become sexually active and need information about contraception and its use, about relationships, and how to make a good choice for the circumstances they're in."[93]

## Pills, condoms, and other contraceptives

The number of teenage girls using a contraceptive during their first intercourse rose dramatically from the early 1980s to 1995—from 48 percent to 78 percent. Teen girls are most likely to use birth control pills (44 percent), condoms (38 percent), and injectables (10 percent). These and other generally safe and effective birth control methods are available to teens through family planning clinics or physicians, generally, but not always, without a parent's consent. Condoms are also available in vending machines, in drugstores, and in some schools.

Condoms (sheaths made of latex, plastic, or animal tissue that cover the erect penis) and diaphragms (small latex caps that cover the cervix and are smeared with spermicide jelly) act as barriers between the sperm and the egg. Female condoms, which are inserted in the vagina, are also available. Birth control pills and long-acting hormone treatments such as Norplant, a method in which a health practitioner inserts capsules in the woman's upper arm, and Depo-Provera, which is given by injection, cause changes in the reproductive system that prevent pregnancy.

*Teen girls who use contraception today are most likely to use birth control pills.*

An alternative is the intrauterine device (IUD), a small apparatus that contains copper or hormones. When inserted in the uterus, the IUD prevents the egg from joining the sperm and from becoming implanted in the uterus. An IUD must be inserted by a medical professional.

Emergency contraception is also available. If an IUD is inserted within five days after unprotected intercourse, there is a 99.9 percent chance of preventing pregnancy. Increased doses of hormonal contraceptive drugs taken within seventy-two hours of unprotected sex are 75 percent effective in preventing pregnancy.

While all of these methods are considered safe for healthy women, side effects have been documented. These may include nausea, spotting between menstrual periods, missed periods, headaches, or blood clots. Smoking while taking the pill and other hormone-based contraceptives can increase the risk of heart attack or stroke.

## A sense of the future

Beyond educational movements to promote abstinence or educate teens about birth control, and perhaps overlapping them, is the notion that larger problems in our society may be at the root of teen pregnancy. In response, broader approaches have been proposed and are being implemented. They may have as their purposes improving the lives of poverty-stricken, poorly educated, or neglected teens; increasing adolescent girls' sense of who they are and what is best for them; and increasing boys' responsibility for sexual relationships and their consequences.

Some programs to combat teen pregnancy are aimed at improving the teenage girl's quality of life. As stated by the National Campaign to Prevent Teen Pregnancy:

> Increasing the capacity of families and communities to nurture teens and help them stay in school and set goals for their lives may contribute to lower rates of teen pregnancy. . . . The definition of what constitutes teen pregnancy prevention is best expanded to include activities that seek to instill teens with confidence and a sense of the future. This speaks to motivation to avoid pregnancy, a critical element in a pregnancy-free adolescence.[94]

*Programs to combat teen pregnancy are sponsored by groups such as the Girl Scouts of America.*

Such programs include those sponsored by the National Collaboration for Youth (NCY), a youth advocacy group of more than thirty organizations (including the Boy Scouts of America, Inc., Girl Scouts of the USA, and the American Red Cross). NCY seeks to promote "youth development," a "process which prepares young people to meet the challenges of adolescence and adulthood through . . . activities and experiences which help them to become socially, morally, emotionally, physically, and cognitively competent."[95] In real-life terms, teenage girls are actively encouraged to grow, learn, and enhance their self-image by taking part in music and the arts, job skills training, literacy training, and community service.

## Positive thinking

In February 2000 the NCY proposed the Younger Americans Act to help young people grow into "fully prepared adults and effective citizens."[96] Under the proposed act, federal and state funds would be used to improve the lives of young people specifically by fostering better relationships between kids and caring adults, creating safe havens with structured activities for kids to go to during non-school hours, improving teens' physical and mental health, and increasing their marketable skills and competencies.

## Empowering girls

To address what it views as the unique problems of adolescent girls, the U.S. Department of Health and Human Services has worked with the Girl Power! campaign since it was formed in 1996. The department explains the goals and reasoning behind the campaign:

> [The goal is to help] girls between the ages of 9 and 14 make the most of their lives. Because studies show that girls at this age have a tendency to neglect their own aspirations and interests, in addition to becoming less physically active, Girl Power! uses a comprehensive approach that addresses both health issues and the topics of self-worth, motivation, and opportunity. Given young girls' increased vulnerability at this stage to negative influences and mixed messages regarding health risk behaviors, the Girl Power! Campaign focuses on increasing their skills and competence in academics, arts, sports, and other beneficial activities. By encouraging girls to develop their skills and sense of self, Girl Power! hopes to decrease the likelihood that they will participate in risky and unhealthy behavior.[97]

Programs that bolster self-esteem may also prevent girls from becoming involved in harmful relationships with older men. In California, where men over twenty father two-thirds of adolescents' babies, discussions along this line have been taking place for a few years. The state increased its budget for prosecution of statutory rape (sexual intercourse with partners too young, by law, to consent to the act). But, as described in the *Los Angeles Times:*

> . . . [F]amily planning experts say the problem goes deeper than anything criminal prosecution alone can resolve. They say that although strict enforcement of statutory rape laws may deter many men, the motivation of younger girls to seek older

partners also needs to be addressed. . . . Jerry Tello, director of the National Latino Fatherhood and Family Institute in Los Angeles, said part of the problem lies in the abusive or neglectful communities where many of these teenagers—both male and female—grow up. "If you live in a violent, stress-related environment, and you don't feel special about yourself, then being close to somebody, even for a moment, is fairly attractive."[98]

## Acknowledging female desire

One author, Michelle Fine, believes that girls are not protecting themselves in sexual situations and need more help than they are getting from typical sex education programs. These programs, Fine argues, "may actually disable young women in their negotiations as sexual subjects"[99] because they reinforce the notion that girls are passive victims of sex rather than responsible actors who should look out for their own best interests.

Fine believes that discussions of sex should include an acknowledgment of teens'—especially girls'—natural sexual urges:

> The naming of desire, pleasure, or sexual entitlement, particularly for females, barely exists in the formal agenda of public schooling on sexuality. When spoken, it is tagged with reminders of "consequences"—emotional, physical, moral, reproductive, and/or financial. A genuine discourse of desire would invite adolescents to explore what feels good and bad, desirable and undesirable, grounded in experiences, needs, and limits.[100]

Educators in New York City conducted a literature-based workshop with the idea that eighth-grade girls could explore their feelings and moral attitudes about sexuality and teen pregnancy in a way that is consistent with Fine's theory:

> [The girls] read and discussed nonfiction and fiction, they interviewed teenage mothers, and in the process, they struggled with some very real issues—whether, during their teenage years, to have sex, get pregnant, and have babies. As part of their inquiry they also wrote, rewrote, and published a booklet for their peers, *Our So-Called Teen Years: Stories about Teenage Pregnancy from the Bronx*, and . . . conducted a

workshop with a group of fifth and sixth grade girls to "mentor" them on the subject.[101]

Through this process the girls found "space in their writing and talking" that helped them express their physical desires and deal with their personal conflicts about sex. Girls expressed those conflicts in a number of ways: through giggles and winks that acknowledged that sexual feelings could be fun; through statements such as "you get those . . . urges"[102] combined with remarks showing that they were struggling to decide what to do with those urges; and through expressing concern about whether they should preach to other girls that it is best to abstain from sex.

*It is important to acknowledge teens' sexual desires and to recognize that both girls and boys bear responsibility for their own behavior.*

## Boys, too

While girls may need help dealing with their sexuality in a way that is best for them, boys need help understanding that they, too, have a stake in preventing teen pregnancy. Linda Feldman wrote in the *Christian Science Monitor:*

> The issue of teen pregnancy usually conjures images of a girl—barely out of elementary school, it seems—with a bulging belly. But for every pregnant girl there's a boy or man who helped put her in that situation. He's "pregnant," too. And, advocates say, males need just as much counseling and attention as females on relationships, pregnancy prevention, and, if a baby is born, responsible parenting.[103]

Experts increasingly acknowledge the importance of including boys in the pregnancy-prevention equation. But boys will not necessarily be comfortable in the same settings as girls. In a clinic in North Hollywood the doors were opened to boys—but none showed up. As a news story reported:

> The few men who did trickle in were accompanying their girlfriends. "And what do they see when they come in? They see all girls in the clinic and *Women's Day* magazines on the table," said Demetrius Navarro, one of the clinic's health educators. "They think, 'This place's not for me.'"

> Program developers . . . learned that they need to hire young male staff members who can relate to other teenagers, and get them involved in the planning process. Outreach workers then need to go where the boys are, hanging out with teenage males at area schools during food breaks and working in discussions of sexual responsibility between shots of basketball.[104]

Although the success of these programs is hard to gauge, Navarro did discover that boys were talking to each other about the issues he had raised with them. Efforts have been made to stimulate these conversations in other "guy-friendly" locations such as boys' clubs, sports clinics—even juvenile detention centers, where teen fathers can be reached to teach them parenting skills. Other programs attempt to reach boys on their own terms. It Takes Two, a Des Moines, Iowa, program, uses stand-up comedy, including a skit on male-female communication called "GI

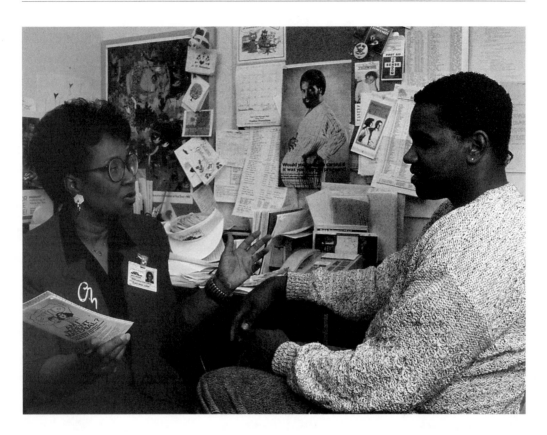

Joe and Barbie Go on a Date." Boys also respond well to positive adult role models, including teachers and fathers.

*A teen receives birth control counseling.*

## Continuing efforts

As the variety of prevention efforts suggests, Americans do not speak in a unified voice about teen sexuality and resulting pregnancies. Moreover, finding effective solutions to teen pregnancy is difficult in a world where the best intentions of boys and girls are challenged. Because they mature younger and marry later, boys and girls have many more years to deal with sexual urges outside of marriage. In addition, they are subjected to many more sexual images in the media than their parents or grandparents were.

As America enters the twenty-first century, it is likely that the debate over the best way to deal with teenage pregnancy will continue, and that the sense of urgency accompanying this debate will not diminish.

# Notes

### *Introduction*

1. Quoted in Don Terry, "Fewer Teen-Age Mothers? Maybe. In Los Angeles They're Skeptical." *New York Times*, May 5, 1998, p. A18(L).

2. Quoted in Beatrice M. Sparks, ed., *It Happened to Nancy: A True Story From Her Diary*. New York: Avon Books, 1994, pp. 116–17.

3. Cynthia Hanson, "Mom, I'm Pregnant," *Ladies' Home Journal*, August 1999, p. 126+.

4. Quoted in Hanson, "Mom, I'm Pregnant."

5. Quoted in Hanson, "Mom, I'm Pregnant."

6. Quoted in Hanson, "Mom, I'm Pregnant."

### *Chapter 1: The Problem with Teen Pregnancy*

7. Planned Parenthood Federation of America, "Sexually Transmitted Infections: The Facts," April 1997. www.plannedparenthood.org/sti-safesex/stifacts--hold.htm.

8. Centers for Disease Control and Prevention, "How long does it take for HIV to cause AIDS?" November 30, 1998. www.cdc.gov/hiv/pubs/faq/faq4.htm.

9. Sparks, *It Happened to Nancy*, pp. 226–27.

10. Sparks, *It Happened to Nancy*, p. 227.

11. Sparks, *It Happened to Nancy*, p. 224.

12. Planned Parenthood Federation of America ("teenwire" warehouse), "Getting Tested for HIV." www.teenwire.com/warehouse/articles/wh_ 19981201p040.asp.

13. Kristin Luker, *Dubious Conceptions: The Politics of Teenage Pregnancy*. Cambridge, MA: Harvard University Press, 1996, p. 118.

14. Luker, *Dubious Conceptions*, p. 107.

15. National Campaign to Prevent Teen Pregnancy, *Get Organized: A Guide to Preventing Teen Pregnancy*, 1999, vol. 1, p. 6.

16. Luker, *Dubious Conceptions*, p. 120.

17. Quoted in David Schaafsma, Antonio Tendero, and Jennifer Tendero, "Making It Real: Girls' Stories, Social Change, and Moral Struggle," *English Journal*, May 28, 1999, p. 31.

18. Quoted in National Campaign to Prevent Teen Pregnancy, "Teen Pregnancy, So What?" www.teenpregnancy.org/sowhat.htm.

19. Quoted in Evelyn Lerman, *Teen Moms: The Pain and the Promise*. Buena Park, CA: Morning Glory Press, 1997, p. 110.

20. Naomi Schaefer, "Honor Society Flunks Out," *Wall Street Journal*, August 28, 1998, p. W11(E).

21. Karen Grigsby Bates, "Choices and Consequences; Rose Court: The tournament is right to bar teenage mothers," *Los Angeles Times*, October 4, 1998.

22. Centers for Disease Control and Prevention, "STDs and Pregnancy," October 1997. www.cdc.gov/nchstp/dstd/Fact_Sheets/facts_stds_and_pregnancy.htm.

23. National Campaign to Prevent Teen Pregnancy, "Teen Pregnancy, So What?"

24. Marie McCullough, "Grossberg case hasn't deterred other pregnant teens, nor explained why," *Knight-Ridder/Tribune News Service*, April 22, 1998, p. 422K3572.

25. Annie E. Casey Foundation, "When Teens Have Sex: Issues and Trends, Overview," April 25, 2000. www.aecf.org/kidscount/teen/overview/overview.htm.

### *Chapter 2: How Does It Happen?*

26. Liza Mundy, "Sex and Sensibility," *Washington Post Online*, July 12, 2000. www.washingtonpost.com/wp-dyn/style/postmagazine/A30405-2000Jul12.html.

27. Jessica B. Gillooly, *Before She Gets Her Period: Talk-*

*ing with Your Daughter about Menstruation.* Los Angeles: Perspective Publishing, 1998, pp. 7–8.

28. National Campaign to Prevent Teen Pregnancy, *Get Organized,* vol. 1, p. 5.

29. Sparks, *It Happened to Nancy,* p. 232.

30. Mundy, "Sex and Sensibility."

31. National Campaign to Prevent Teen Pregnancy, *Get Organized,* vol. 1, p. 5.

32. SarahYang, "Pregnancy Prevention Targets Males," *Los Angeles Times,* June 24, 1998, p. B-1+.

33. Quoted in "The Naked Truth," *Newsweek,* May 8, 2000, p. 59.

34. Anna Runkle, *In Good Conscience: A Practical, Emotional, and Spiritual Guide to Deciding Whether to Have an Abortion.* San Francisco: Jossey-Bass Publishers, 1998, p. 92.

35. Quoted in Mundy, "Sex and Sensibility."

36. Quoted in Lois Weis and Michelle Fine, eds., *Beyond Silenced Voices: Class, Race, and Gender in United States Schools.* Albany: State University of New York Press, 1993, p. 82.

37. Mundy, "Sex and Sensibility."

38. Quoted in Lerman, *Teen Moms,* p. 135.

39. Quoted in Lerman, *Teen Moms,* pp. 137–38.

40. Quoted in Weis and Fine, *Beyond Silenced Voices,* p. 84.

41. Leon Dash, *When Children Want Children: The Urban Crisis of Teenage Childbearing.* New York: William Morrow and Company, Inc., 1989, p. 9.

42. Jane Pratt and Kelli Pryor, *For Real: The Uncensored Truth About America's Teenagers.* New York: Hyperion, 1995, p. 183.

43. Yang, "Pregnancy Prevention Targets Males."

44. Yang, "Pregnancy Prevention Targets Males."

45. Mundy, "Sex and Sensibility."

46. Oliver Starr Jr., "Teen Girls Are Easy Prey for Over-20 Predators," *Insight on the News,* May 3, 1999, vol. 15, i16, p. 28(1)+.

47. Quoted in Starr, "Teen Girls Are Easy Prey for Over-20 Predators."

48. Quoted in Schaafsma, Tendero, and Tendero, "Making It Real," p. 34.

49. Brian Lowry, "WB Covers a Trend Too Well: When Sexy Women Portray Teens, What Messages are Conveyed to Young Viewers?" *Los Angeles Times*, June 20, 2000, p. F1.

50. Quoted in "The Naked Truth," p. 59.

51. Gary Thomas, "Where True Love Waits," *Christianity Today*, March 1, 1999, p. 40(1)+.

52. Quoted in Thomas, "Where True Love Waits," p. 40.

### *Chapter 3: Coming to Terms with Parenthood*

53. Sheila Kitzinger, *The Complete Book of Pregnancy and Childbirth*. New York: Alfred A. Knopf, 1996, p. 140.

54. William Sears and Martha Sears with Linday Hughey Holt, *The Pregnancy Book: A Month-by-Month Guide*. Boston: Little, Brown and Company, 1997, p. 96.

55. National Campaign to Prevent Teen Pregnancy, "Teen Pregnancy, So What?"

56. Sears and Sears, *The Pregnancy Book*, p. 45.

57. Sears and Sears, *The Pregnancy Book*, pp. 48–49.

58. Quoted in Jeanne Warren Lindsay and Jean Brunelli, *Your Pregnancy and Newborn Journey*. Buena Park, CA: Morning Glory Press, 1994, p. 23.

59. Miriam Stoppard, *Sex Ed: Growing Up, Relationships, and Sex*. New York: DK Publishing, Inc., 1997, p. 78.

60. Quoted in Jeanne Warren Lindsay and Sharon Githens Enright, *Books, Babies, and School-Age Parents: How to Teach Pregnant and Parenting Teens to Succeed*. Buena Park, CA: Morning Glory Press, 1997, p. 138.

61. Elinor B. Rosenberg, *The Adoption Life Cycle: The Children and Their Families Through the Years*. New York: The Free Press, 1992, p. 19.

62. Lindsay and Enright, *Books, Babies, and School-Age Parents*, pp. 117, 199.

63.  Quoted in Karen Gravelle and Leslie Peterson, *Teenage Fathers*. New York: Julian Messner, 1992, p. 64.

64.  Runkle, *In Good Conscience*, pp. 128–29.

65.  Runkle, *In Good Conscience*, p. 129.

### *Chapter 4: Adoption and Abortion*

66.  Ann Farmer, "Tell It to the Judge: Teens Face Hard Times," *Reproductive Freedom News* 8, vol. 8, no. 8, 1999, p. 1+.

67.  Quoted in Farmer, "Tell It to the Judge."

68.  Quoted in Marcia Custer, "Adoption As An Option for Unmarried Pregnant Teens," *Adolescence* 28, no. 112 (Winter 1993), p. 896.

69.  Alan Guttmacher Institute, "Minors and the Right to Consent to Health Care," October 11, 2000. www.agi-usa.org/pubs/ib_minors_oo.html.

70.  Quoted in Rosenberg, *The Adoption Life Cycle*, p. 27.

71.  Quoted in Custer, "Adoption As An Option," pp. 896–97.

72.  Quoted in Shirley Arthur, *Surviving Teen Pregnancy: Your Choices, Dreams, and Decisions*. Buena Park, CA: Morning Glory Press, 1996, p. 91.

73.  Quoted in Aliza Sherman, *Everything You Need to Know about Placing Your Baby for Adoption*, New York: The Rosen Publishing Group, Inc., 1997, p. 37.

74.  Quoted in Custer, "Adoption As An Option," p. 900.

75.  Quoted in Rosenberg, *The Adoption Life Cycle*, pp. 24–25.

76.  Quoted in Lindsay and Enright, *Books, Babies, and School-Age Parents*, p. 174.

77.  Lois Gilman, *The Adoption Resource Book*. New York: HarperPerennial, 1998, p. 111.

78.  Gilman, *The Adoption Resource Book*, p. 116.

79.  Quoted in Runkle, *In Good Conscience*, pp. 49–50.

80.  Quoted in Gilman, *The Adoption Resource Book*, p. 133.

81. Quoted in Gilman, *The Adoption Resource Book*, p. 113.

82. Quoted in Rosenberg, *The Adoption Life Cycle*, p. 38.

### *Chapter 5: Approaches to the Problem*

83. Annie E. Casey Foundation, "2000 Kids Count Data Online," June 19, 2000. www.aecf.org/kidscount/kc2000/sum_7.htm.

84. National Campaign to Prevent Teen Pregnancy, "What the Polling Data Tell Us: A Summary of Past Surveys on Teen Pregnancy," April 1997. www.teenpregnancy.org/Polling.htm.

85. Quoted in Marilyn Gardner, "Shifts in Sex Ed: Talking Abstinence," *Christian Science Monitor*, August 11, 1998, p. B7.

86. Quoted in Gardner, "Shifts in Sex Ed: Talking Abstinence," pp. B1 and B7.

87. Quoted in Gardner, "Shifts in Sex Ed: Talking Abstinence," p. B7.

88. Quoted in Thomas, "Where True Love Waits."

89. Quoted in National Campaign to Prevent Teen Pregnancy, "What the Polling Data Tell Us."

90. Annie E. Casey Foundation, "Plain Talk," April 24, 2000. www.aecf.org/publications/plaintalk/p1-atlanta.htm.

91. Quoted in National Campaign to Prevent Teen Pregnancy, "What the Polling Data Tell Us."

92. Quoted in Gardner, "Shifts in Sex Ed: Talking Abstinence," p. B7.

93. Quoted in Gardner, "Shifts in Sex Ed: Talking Abstinence," p. B7.

94. National Campaign to Prevent Teen Pregnancy, *Get Organized*, vol. 1, p. 7.

95. National Youth Development Information Center, "Definitions of Youth Development," 2000. www.nydic.org/devdef.html.

96. National Youth Development Information Center, "Younger Americans Act," 2001. www.nydic.org/YAA.html.

97. U.S. Department of Health and Human Services, "A National Strategy to Prevent Teen Pregnancy," 1999. http://aspe.os. dhhs.gov/hsp/teenp/teenpreg99.htm.

98. Yang, "Pregnancy Prevention Targets Males."

99. Weis and Fine, *Beyond Silenced Voices*, p. 90.

100. Weis and Fine, *Beyond Silenced Voices*, p. 79.

101. Quoted in Schaafsma, Tendero, and Tendero, "Making It Real," p. 28.

102. Quoted in Schaafsma, Tendero, and Tendero, "Making It Real," p 35.

103. Linda Feldman, "Targeting Boys in Fight Against Teen Pregnancy," *Christian Science Monitor*, January 7, 1998, p. 1.

104. Yang, "Pregnancy Prevention Targets Males."

# Organizations to Contact

The following organizations can be contacted for additional information on teen pregnancy.

AIDS and STD information:
Centers for Disease Control and Prevention,
National STD and AIDS Hotline: 1-800-342-2437

Provides information and referrals twenty-four hours a day/seven days a week.

**Annie E. Casey Foundation**
701 St. Paul Street
Baltimore, Maryland 21202
Phone: 800-222-1099
Fax: 410-547-6624
Website: www.aecf.org
E-Mail: webmail@aecf.org

This foundation supports public and private initiatives to improve the lives of at-risk kids. It also provides grants and compiles and analyzes information relevant to its goals.

**National Abstinence Clearinghouse (N.A.C.)**
801 East 41st Street
Sioux Falls, SD 57105
Phone: 888-577-2966
Fax: 605-335-0629
Website: www.abstinence.net
E-mail: info@abstinence.net

N.A.C. distributes materials to promote abstinence until marriage.

**National Adoption Information Clearinghouse (N.A.I.C.)**
330 C Street, SW
Washington, DC 20447
Phone: 888-251-0075
Fax: 703-385-3206
Website: www.calib.com/naic

N.A.I.C. distributes information on adoption.

**National Campaign to Prevent Teen Pregnancy**
1776 Massachusetts Avenue, NW, Suite 200
Washington, DC 20036
Phone: 202-478-8500
Fax: 202-478-8588
Website: www.teenpregnancy.org
E-mail: campaign@teenpregnancy.org

The campaign's goal is to reduce teen pregnancy by one-third by the year 2005. The campaign promotes this goal through media campaigns, contact with community leaders, and publication of reports and action guides.

**Planned Parenthood Federation of America**
810 Seventh Avenue
New York, NY 10019
Phone: 800-829-7732
Website: www.plannedparenthood.org
           www.teenwire.com
E-mail: communications@ppfa.org

Planned Parenthood is the oldest and largest organization supporting voluntary family planning. It provides reproductive services at health centers, compiles research, and lobbies to promote its goals.

# Suggestions for Further Reading

## Books

Shirley Arthur, *Surviving Teen Pregnancy: Your Choices, Dreams, and Decisions.* Buena Park, CA: Morning Glory Press, 1996. Practical advice on options and where to find help.

Janet Bode, *Kids Still Having Kids: Talking About Teen Pregnancy.* Danbury, CT: Franklin Watts, 1999. Easy-to-follow discussions by teens, their families, health care workers, and counselors.

Robert W. Buckingham and Mary P. Derby, *"I'm Pregnant, Now What Do I Do?"* Amherst, NY: Prometheus Books, 1997. Excellent, detailed, but readable resource for teens facing pregnancy.

Andrea Engber and Leah Klungness, *The Complete Single Mother.* Holbrook, MA: Adams Publishing, 1995. Comprehensive coverage of practical, legal, and social issues of single mothering and child development. Includes information that will be helpful to teen mothers as they become adults.

Evelyn Lerman, *Teen Moms: The Pain and the Promise.* Buena Park, CA: Morning Glory Press, 1997. Touching personal accounts mixed with solid information about the causes of teen pregnancy and possible ways of reducing it.

Jeanne Warren Lindsay, *Expectations and Reality: Teen Views on Living Together, Roles, Work, Jealousy, and Partner Abuse.* Buena Park, CA: Morning Glory Press,

1996. Results of interviews with nearly four thousand teens, showing ten-year trends in attitudes.

Jeanne Warren Lindsay and Jean Brunelli, *Your Pregnancy and Newborn Journey.* Buena Park, CA: Morning Glory Press, 1994. Personal and practical account of teen pregnancy.

Barbara Moe, *Everything You Need to Know About Sexual Abstinence.* New York: The Rosen Publishing Group, Inc., 1996. Describes how to evaluate and implement a choice to be sexually abstinent, including practical, youth-friendly sample situations and dialogues.

Jane Pratt and Kelli Pryor, *For Real: The Uncensored Truth About America's Teenagers.* New York: Hyperion, 1995. Helpful insights into real teens' attitudes about sex and pregnancy.

Aliza Sherman, *Everything You Need to Know about Placing Your Baby for Adoption.* New York: The Rosen Publishing Group, Inc., 1997. Easy to read and informative summary of the adoption process.

Gail B. Stewart, *Teen Parenting.* San Diego: Lucent Books, Inc., 2000. A helpful overview of the issues, with a focus on girls' personal experiences.

Stephen P. Thompson, ed., *Teenage Pregnancy: Opposing Viewpoints.* San Diego: Greenhaven Press, Inc., 1997. Well-explained, balanced selection of writings on the problem, and proposed solutions.

## Websites

www.iwannaknow.org. Website of the American Social Health Association that provides youth-oriented information and a chat room for questions.

# Works Consulted

**Books**

Leon Dash, *When Children Want Children: The Urban Crisis of Teenage Childbearing*. New York: William Morrow and Company, Inc., 1989. Personal accounts of pregnant teens in the Washington, D.C., area.

Jessica B. Gillooly, *Before She Gets Her Period: Talking with Your Daughter about Menstruation*. Los Angeles: Perspective Publishing, 1998. Includes a section on the trend toward early menstruation.

Lois Gilman, *The Adoption Resource Book*. New York: HarperPerennial, 1998. Highly recommended practical and personal guide.

Karen Gravelle and Leslie Peterson, *Teenage Fathers*. New York: Julian Messner, 1992. Insightful case studies of teen fathers.

Sheila Kitzinger, *The Complete Book of Pregnancy and Childbirth*. New York: Alfred A. Knopf, 1996. Comprehensive treatment of pregnancy and childbirth.

Jeanne Warren Lindsay and Sharon Githens Enright, *Books, Babies, and School-Age Parents: How to Teach Pregnant and Parenting Teens To Succeed*. Buena Park, CA: Morning Glory Press, 1997. Aimed at educators, this book is a challenging read on current thinking about supporting pregnant teens socially and educationally.

Kristin Luker, *Dubious Conceptions: The Politics of Teenage Pregnancy*. Cambridge, MA: Harvard University Press, 1996. A challenging look at how Americans view and deal with teen pregnancy.

National Campaign to Prevent Teen Pregnancy, *Get Organized: A Guide to Preventing Teen Pregnancy*, 1999. A comprehensive guide for groups launching teen pregnancy programs.

Elinor B. Rosenberg, *The Adoption Life Cycle: The Children and Their Families Through the Years*. New York: The Free Press, 1992. Touching insight into the realities of adoption.

Anna Runkle, *In Good Conscience: A Practical, Emotional, and Spiritual Guide to Deciding Whether to Have an Abortion*. San Francisco: Jossey-Bass Publishers, 1998. A workbook with meaningful exercises on whether an abortion is the best course of action. Includes a discussion of the politics of abortion and real-life experiences.

William Sears and Martha Sears with Linda Hughey Holt, *The Pregnancy Book: A Month-by-Month Guide*. Boston: Little, Brown and Company, 1997. Excellent, complete guide with readable explanations.

Beatrice M. Sparks, ed., *It Happened to Nancy: A True Story From Her Diary*. New York: Avon Books, 1994. An emotionally difficult, true account of a teen's death after contracting AIDS as a result of a date rape.

Miriam Stoppard, *Sex Ed: Growing Up, Relationships, and Sex*. New York: DK Publishing, Inc., 1997. A straightforward "how-to" book that includes a helpful summary of the social and emotional aspects of sexuality.

Lois Weis and Michelle Fine, eds., *Beyond Silenced Voices: Class, Race, and Gender in United States Schools*. Albany: State University of New York Press, 1993. A more difficult book that includes a chapter exploring how American girls should be taught about sexuality.

## Periodicals and Internet Sources

Alan Guttmacher Institute, "Minors and the Right to Consent to Health Care," October 11, 2000. www.agi-usa.org/pubs/ib_minors_oo.html.

Annie E. Casey Foundation, "Plain Talk," April 24, 2000. www.aecf.org/publications/plaintalk/p1-atlanta.htm.

Annie E. Casey Foundation, "2000 Kids Count Data Online," June 19, 2000. www.aecf.org/kidscount/kc2000/sum_7.htm.

Annie E. Casey Foundation, "When Teens Have Sex: Issues and Trends, Overview," April 25, 2000. www.aecf.org/kidscount/teen/overview/overview.htm.

Karen Grigsby Bates, "Choices and Consequences; Rose Court: The tournament is right to bar teenage mothers," *Los Angeles Times*, October 4, 1998.

Centers for Disease Control and Prevention, "How long does it take for HIV to cause AIDS?" November 30, 1998. www.cdc.gov/hiv/pubs/faq/faq4.htm.

Centers for Disease Control and Prevention, "STDs and Pregnancy," October 1997. www.cdc.gov/nchstp/dstd/Fact_Sheets/facts_stds_and_pregnancy.htm.

Marcia Custer, "Adoption As An Option for Unmarried Pregnant Teens," *Adolescence* 28, no. 112, winter 1993.

Ann Farmer, "Tell It to the Judge: Teens Face Hard Times," *Reproductive Freedom News* 8, no. 8, 1999.

Linda Feldman, "Targeting Boys in Fight Against Teen Pregnancy," *Christian Science Monitor*, January 7, 1998.

Marilyn Gardner, "Shifts in Sex Ed: Talking Abstinence," *Christian Science Monitor*, August 11, 1998.

Cynthia Hanson, "Mom, I'm Pregnant," *Ladies' Home Journal*, August 1999.

Brian Lowry, "WB Covers a Trend Too Well: When Sexy Women Portray Teens, What Messages are Conveyed to Young Viewers?" *Los Angeles Times*, June 20, 2000.

Marie McCullough, "Grossberg case hasn't deterred other

pregnant teens, nor explained why," *Knight-Ridder/Tribune News Service*, April 22, 1998.

Liza Mundy, "Sex and Sensibility," *Washington Post Online*, July 12, 2000. www.washingtonpost.com/wp-dyn/style/postmagazine/A30405-2000Jul12.html.

"The Naked Truth," *Newsweek*, May 8, 2000.

National Campaign to Prevent Teen Pregnancy, "Teen Pregnancy, So What?" www.teenpregnancy.org/sowhat.htm.

National Campaign to Prevent Teen Pregnancy, "What the Polling Data Tell Us: A Summary of Past Surveys on Teen Pregnancy," April 1997. www.teenpregnancy.org/Polling.htm.

National Youth Development Information Center, "Definitions of Youth Development," 2000. www.nydic.org/devdef.html.

National Youth Development Information Center, "Younger Americans Act," 2001. www.nydic.org/YAA.html.

Planned Parenthood Federation of America, "Sexually Transmitted Infections: The Facts," April 1997. www.plannedparenthood.org/sti-safesex/stifacts--hold.htm.

Planned Parenthood Federation of America ("teenwire" warehouse), "Getting Tested for HIV." www.teenwire.com/warehouse/articles/wh_19981201p040.asp.

David Schaafsma, Antonio Tendero, and Jennifer Tendero, "Making It Real: Girls' Stories, Social Change, and Moral Struggle," *English Journal*, May 28, 1999.

Naomi Schaefer, "Honor Society Flunks Out," *Wall Street Journal*, August 28, 1998.

Oliver Starr Jr., "Teen Girls Are Easy Prey for Over-20 Predators," *Insight on the News*, May 3, 1999.

Don Terry, "Fewer Teen-Age Mothers? Maybe," *New York Times*, May 5, 1998.

Gary Thomas, "Where True Love Waits," *Christianity Today*, March 1, 1999.

U.S. Department of Health and Human Services, "A National Strategy to Prevent Teen Pregnancy," 1999. http://aspe.os.dhhs. gov/hsp/teenp/teenpreg99.htm.

Sarah Yang, "Pregnancy Prevention Targets Males," *Los Angeles Times*, June 24, 1998.

# Index

parenting skills of, 24–26
teen pregnancy
causes of, 17–19
costs of, for society, 26–27
debate over, 10
decisions in, 7–10
decline in, 6–7
emotions surrounding, 7–8
family reaction to, 49
health risks of, 16–17
intentional, 12, 34–38
personal responsibility and, 11–12
prevention of, 72–85
  abstinence programs, 73–75
  acknowledging desire and, 82–83
  boys' role in, 84–85
  comprehensive programs for, 77
  contraceptives, 77–79
  empowering girls and, 81–82
  improving quality of teens' lives and, 79–81
  parental communication, 75–76
as rite of passage, 35–38

society's opposition to, 11–12
in United States, 71
see also pregnancy
teen sexuality
  conflicting messages about, 31–32
  early sexual maturity and, 30
  female desire and, 82–83
  lack of maturity and, 28
  marriage age and, 29–30
  peer pressure and, 40–42
  role of drugs and alcohol in, 30–31
see also sexual activity
television shows, 39–40
Terry, Don, 6
Thomas, Gary, 40–42

United States, teen pregnancy in, 71
U.S. Supreme Court, abortion and, 59–61

welfare, 57–58
Williams, John, 38
Woods, Cathi, 40–41, 75

Yang, Sarah, 32

# Picture Credits

Cover photo: © Elaine Rebman/Photo Researchers, Inc.
Nina Berman/ SIPA, 63
CC Studio/Science Photo Library/Photo Researchers, Inc., 12
© Ron Chapple 1993/FPG, 66
Jeff Christensen/SIPA, 41
© Spencer Grant/Photo Researchers, Inc., 51
© Michael Hart 1996/FPG, 48
Ansell Horn/Impact Visuals, 45
© Richard Hutchings/Photo Researchers, Inc., 21
© Susan Kuklin 1990/Photo Researchers, Inc., 37
© Andy Levin 1992/Photo Researchers, Inc., 18
© Jeff Lowenthal/Woodfin Camp, 78
© Robert Maass/Corbis, 72
© Ursula Markus/Photo Researchers, Inc., 29
©Stephanie Maze/Corbis, 68
© Richard T. Nowitz/Corbis, 80
A. Ortega/SIPA, 40
© Alexandra Pais/Impact Visuals, 36
© Caroline Penn/Corbis, 56
Photo Researchers, Inc., 76
© A. Ramey/Woodfin Camp, 54, 57
© Reuters NewMedia, Inc./Corbis, 74
© Blair Seitz 1987/Photo Researchers, Inc., 14
© Kathy Sloane 1993/Photo Researchers, Inc., 53
© J. Gerard Smith/Photo Researchers, Inc., 22
© Erika Stone/Photo Researchers, Inc., 70
© Telegraph Colour Library 1998/FPG International, 60
© Telegraph Colour Library 1997/FPG International, 31
© Arthur Tress/Photo Researchers, Inc., 19
© VCG 1999/FPG International, 25
© Steve Wewerka/Impact Visuals, 9
© 1997 Jim West/Impact Visuals, 8
© James Wilson/Woodfin Camp, 85
© Jennie Woodcock/Reflections Photolibrary/Corbis, 34
© Michael Wray/Corbis, 83

# About the Author

Patrice Cassedy is the author of *Understanding Flowers for Algernon* (Lucent Books) and many articles for magazines. She has worked as a literary magazine editor and consumer credit attorney. Cassedy is married and has two children. She and her family enjoy oceanside walks and attending jazz and classical music concerts. Cassedy spent a year in Washington, D.C., where she visited museums and historical sites.